GREAT ITALIAN AMERICAN FOOD IN NEW ENGLAND

For
Eleanor
"Buon appetit"
John Carafoli

GREAT
Italian American
FOOD
IN NEW ENGLAND
HISTORY, TRADITIONS & MEMORIES

JOHN F. CARAFOLI

PHOTOGRAPHY BY FRANCINE ZASLOW

Globe
Pequot

GUILFORD, CONNECTICUT

This book would not have been possible if I had not been born
and brought up in the small village of Sagamore on Cape Cod.
It was truly an Italian-American community.

Globe
Pequot

An imprint of Rowman & Littlefield
Distributed by NATIONAL BOOK NETWORK

Copyright © 2016 by John F. Carafoli
Photography © Francine Zaslow unless otherwise noted
Design by Nancy Freeborn

British Library Cataloguing in Publication Information Available

Library of Congress Cataloging-in-Publication Data Available

ISBN 978-1-4930-1644-0 (paperback)
ISBN 978-1-4930-2524-4 (e-book)

♾™ The paper used in this publication meets the minimum requirements of American National Standard
for Information Sciences—Permanence of Paper for Printed Library Materials, ANSI/NISO Z39.48-1992.

CONTENTS

WHY DO RECIPES MATTER?

BY ANNE MENDELSON

As a culinary historian, I'm used to fielding that question from a detective standpoint involving written clues about how one-time luxuries trickled down to the middle class or when tofu went mainstream. It's easy to forget that there are answers linked to a completely different realm of experience. People's memories and associations are also a kind of history: subjective, intangible annals that we carry around within ourselves but often feel compelled to share with someone else in objective, tangible ways.

What could be a more impossible-to-communicate private history than any person's experience of food? What could be harder to convey through words than the tastes and smells of fish frying or raspberries being crushed for a sauce, the tactile sensations of dough being worked? And beyond that, what could be more elusive and swifter to vanish than the moments people spend eating in each other's company?

No recipe has ever existed that could fully realize any of this. Recipes are a seriously imperfect means of teaching anyone to cook. But that doesn't mean that they're wasted labor. In fact, by my lights, some women and men with no ties to professional food-writing circles who try to communicate the making of dishes that mean something to them, and by implication people they care about, can be the most wonderful recipe writers of all.

My friend Cara De Silva, who has spent decades exploring records of how inmates of prison camps have talked or even written about food, relates that at Auschwitz women would shout recipes for beloved dishes over the fence to women in the next compound. What could make anyone do such a thing except sheer will to salvage some living bit of family and community from the wreck of everything? To say, "Here is a part of us you can't destroy," by the act of passing it on to be kept alive in the hearts of others?

Luckier people have left old lives and built new ones while maintaining the floodways that meant family and community for them. Such was the case with the Italian immigrants to New England whose cooking John Carafoli documents in this book. The enclaves they founded from Maine to Connecticut are almost gone today, but the culinary birthright of the first generation had great staying power in the hearts and minds of at least some descendants.

Italian-born people whose only recipes lay in their memories and fingertips survived to share their skills with cookbook-using children or grandchildren. And today some of those later generations are determined to use recipes to say, like the women in the concentration camps, "This is a piece of what we were and are. It's our duty to bequeath it."

No, recipes can't fully resurrect the living past. But they can reach back into it with love and loyalty.

Anne Mendelson is a culinary historian and author of *Stand Facing the Stove: The Story of the Women Who Gave America The Joy of Cooking, Milk: The Surprising Story of Milk through the Ages,* and *Chow Chop Suey: Food and the Chinese American Journey.*

INTRODUCTION

With the writing of this book, I have been fortunate to meet many Italian-Americans throughout New England who experienced their heritage much as I did growing up in post-war Sagamore Beach. Many still want, as I do, to perpetuate now nearly lost family traditions. Some of these traditions were things they experienced directly, others were handed down as family lore. Among Italian immigrants, the family played a major and complex role, both in America and back in the "old country," Italy. In America the family gave immigrants a sense of security in an unfamiliar land. Their traditions, family ties, friends, and community created a bond that kept them together. Today, Italians love to reminisce about their experiences growing up. This book samples and explores the Italian heritage in New England. It is a cookbook with history, interviews, memories, special features, and recipes from Italian-Americans.

The Five hundred Italians digging the Cape Cod Cannel late 1800's.

The Cecchi family with John and Maria in front.

My research started with a call to a distant relative in Plymouth, Massachusetts, who told me about Plymouth native Marlene Brigida Baldwin who wrote a cookbook memoir called *Nonna's Cucina and Beyond: A collection of Recipes and Anecdotes* (see page 116). I contacted Marlene in her current home in Keene, New Hampshire. She then put me in touch with her cousin Joan Zechi, who lives in Springfield, Massachusetts, and through Joan I met Rose Palazzi (see page 118) and visited Balboni's Bakery (see page 90), and that led to another meeting and another until I had built a network of individuals who guided me through the six New England states connected by their common desire to preserve a rich and wonderful heritage. Community is what this book is about.

My grandfather Lugi, grandmother Inez, and me at age four.

* * *

In 1880, between 450 and 500 Italian laborers traveled from New York to Cape Cod, specifically Sagamore and Sandwich, to dig the Cape Cod Canal with picks and shovels. They were never paid by the Cape Cod Canal Company, or even fed during the last few weeks. Some laborers roamed the town looking for food and work, but since they spoke no English, they were feared by Cape Codders who didn't understand them and thought them dangerous.

In the early 1900s the Keith Car Manufacturing Company, makers of railroad cars, was hiring workers. Many of the very same men who had helped dig the canal were now joined by their relatives who had arrived from Italy also in search of employment and found work there. Coming to a foreign land and not speaking the language, they settled in a large apartment complex known as "The Blocks," where they spoke Italian to each other and cooked the familiar dishes of their native land while adapting to the new ingredients here.

Later, other immigrants, mostly from Northern Italy, settled in Sagamore looking for a better life. My grandparents, who already had relatives here, were among them. I grew up in Sagamore in the late 1940s and 1950s. It was then a tightly-knit Italian-American community on the Cape Cod side of the canal. During my childhood and adolescence, year-round residents lived in the village, but for three months, we were joined by the "exclusive" summer people from Boston who lived in beachfront cottages in Sagamore Beach, across the bridge on the mainland. We were "the townies," and did not belong to that community. The village proper turned quiet and serene in the fall when the summer people left. In the fall, St. Therese's Catholic Church and a few stores again established themselves as the center of many Italian community activities. They hosted spaghetti suppers, penny and tag sales, pancake breakfasts, and even small talent shows. The church was also the place where the village people were baptized and married and from which they were buried. Louis Market was the hub for news and gossip. In the cellar of the market was a bakery that made the famous bread from Northern Italy, referred to as "horn" or "star" bread. I remember when I was six running to the bakery on a Saturday morning for fresh dough that my mother fashioned into sweet, fried "doughboys" made with her special cookie cutter and dusted with cinnamon sugar. This was a real treat.

My mother Helena, father John, and I lived with my grandparents, Inez and Lugi, and Aunt Mary. I was the first child born into the family. Living with my grandparents was the happiest time of my childhood. Always, a variety of foods were being prepared and eaten in my grandparents' home. My grandmother, like all Italian mothers, was a nurturer. She created love through her food and in return received love from the people who ate it.

My grandmother's kitchen made a lasting impression on me, it was my playpen. I especially recall the large, round family table with the lion claw legs centered in the middle of the kitchen, on top of the 1940s linoleum. One wall housed my grandmother's late-1800s maple Hoosier cabinet where she created wonderful family dinners with homemade pasta. I watched her roll out pasta with a large rolling pin that was longer than I was tall at the time. Sometimes I would hide under the cabinet while she made the pasta and watch some of the flour fall to the floor like snow in front of me. Only

Me at age six

good feelings and happy times were associated with that kitchen. Most of all, I remember the smells and aromas emanating from her homemade sauces, cacciatores that cooked on the stove for hours, and her hearty chicken soup that she would ladle from the pot and whip an egg into and feed me when I was sick. I remember, too, her preserving fresh tomatoes for the winter months when she would use them in her sauces. Today as I make her chicken soup and pasta recipes, preserve my tomatoes, and smell the wood of her Hoosier cabinet that is now in my kitchen, I realize how richly she shaped my life.

My grandmother picked spring's first dandelions. I remember her sitting on an ornate cement bench under the crabapple tree in the backyard sorting the dandelions she had gathered in her handmade flowered apron, and washing them in a large bowl of water that she changed several times under the outside faucet. At dinnertime she would make a dandelion and hard-cooked egg salad. The dressing was a simple oil

Leanardo "Nello" Belegno;
Laura Borghi; Sisters Yolanda
Tavares & Madeleine Dante;
a cookbook put out by the
ladies of Sagamore 1978.

WHAT'S COOKING IN SAGAMORE?

SAGAMORE MOTHERS CLUB

and red wine vinegar, made from my grandfather's wine. Her ornate cement bench, now on the patio near my herb garden, keeps this memory before me.

My grandfather was also a great influence on me. He had a wine cellar filled with winemaking equipment. Rows of red wine lined the walls. Frequent trips to the wine cellar with him were lovely times. He would take me by the hand, assuring me it was safe as he led me down the narrow stairs. The cellar was cool, dark, and had a musty fermented grape fragrance. It was lit with a lonely light bulb hanging from a wire, attached to the ceiling next to the furnace. On some occasions I sat on the bottom cellar step while my grandfather cooked a steak over the coals in the furnace for the family supper. When he was finished, he would go to the racks of wine, select one, and we would be on our way back up the stairs. In the kitchen, he would open the wine with an old brass corkscrew and take two glasses from the cupboard; in one he put a teaspoon of sugar, then poured the wine over it and stirred it gently. He then sat in his favorite chair at the end of the Hoosier cabinet, picked me up, and perched me on his lap. Placing the wine with the sugar in front of me, he would hand me an end piece of "horn" bread, which I dunked in the wine. My grandfather and grand-mother died before I turned six, but I hold their memories deep in my heart.

I was still young when we moved up the hill to our own home. Five years later my life changed drastically. Shortly after midnight one Saturday in the middle of June the smell of smoke awakened me. I ran to my mother's bed to wake her up. The next thing I saw was a wall of fire shooting up the staircase. Grabbing my one-year-old brother from his crib, I fled out my bedroom window to the roof and yelled to my six-year-old brother Ronny to come to the window. After working late, my father came down the street to find two of his sons on the roof and the rest of his family being consumed by flames. My mother, my invalid grandmother, and Ronny never made it to the roof. Within moments my life fell apart. It would never be the same. All I had left were the pajamas I was wearing and my memories. Out of a desperate need for survival, I went inward, into fantasy, using memories, good feelings, and the experience I had of food as my solace and foundation. It nourished me physically, mentally, and emotionally.

This book will focus on the period that follows when my father, my younger brother Richard, and I moved back to the home I had left five years before. My Aunt

CUNSA

(Herb and Spice Rub)

Cunsa is a rub that is wonderful on meat and poultry. There is not standard formula. All the Sagamore Italian Ladies had their own variations, and proportions are more by feel than measurements. Some added a little uncooked salt port to the mixture, mincing it together with the herbs. See recipe for Chicken under a Brick on page 145.

Course salt

Garlic

Thyme, Parsley

Black crushed pepper

Cloves

Allspice

Bay leaves

Sprig of rosemary

Put a couple of good handfuls of course salt in a small jar with a tight screw top lid.

With a sharp, heavy knife or a mezzaluna, chop together several garlic cloves, a small bunch of fresh thyme, and half a handful of Italian parsley until very finely minced. Add several large pinches of cracked or coarsely ground black pepper; 4 cloves, crushed; 2 to 3 allspice, crushed; and a couple of crushed bay leaves. Some women add a minced sprig of rosemary. Put the lid on the jar and shake vigorously to mix. Some kept the *cunsa* at room temperature and would reach for a pinch as needed. I store it in the refrigerator. It will keep for up to 6 months. (The thing to watch for is moisture getting into it and dissolving the salt getting it wet)

To avoid this, spread the mixture out in a small pan or cookie sheet, put in a 200°F oven for 30 minutes or slightly longer to dry the mixture out. It can then be stored in a jar at room temperature without concern for moisture.

Mary, who was a schoolteacher, still lived there. My father owned and worked in a grain, coal, and feed store in Sandwich. My brother had a sitter until I came home from school. My job, at age eleven, was to mind my baby brother after school. This heavy responsibility forced maturity on me, depriving me of carefree afternoons playing with other children. Being an inquisitive child and looking for things to do, I soon found myself gravitating toward the neighborhood kitchens where my brother and I were welcomed. As much as the fragrant aromas coming from the back doors enticed me, so did the warm hospitality of the women who spent so much of their time over their stoves.

One woman in particular became a surrogate mother, filling a little of the loneliness left by the death of my own mother. Another neighbor piqued my curiosity and interest in mushrooms. One morning I saw Rosina, a slight women in an apron, her gray hair pulled back in a bun, coming home from the woods with a basket of wild mushrooms. I followed her inside and watched her prepare these exotic-looking fungi for the family's supper. Into the saucepan with a little olive oil went the clean mushrooms with a silver dollar, a sprig of parsley, and a slice of white bread. When I asked Rosina to explain this, she shared the folklore in broken English. "If the silver tarnishes and the parsley turns a strange color, the mushrooms are no good."

"But what about the bread?" I asked.

She threw up her hands in a typical Italian manner, and said, "You feed the bread to the chicken. If the chicken dies, your throw the mushrooms out!"

Knowing Rosina and another woman in the neighborhood, Alba Papi, that makes me feel secure in gathering mushrooms today. However, still I am very cautious when foraging for these delectable *fungi*.

I watched these skilled women—some immigrants from the old country, others first-generation Italian-Americans—as I had watched my grandmother a few years before prepare red sauces; cream sauces; a variety of cacciatores made with sausages, pork chops, chicken, or veal; risottos of all descriptions; polenta; and stuffed squid.

I have gathered recipes from the women in the village. In some instances, the recipes come from their daughters, illustrating the strong sense of family and community in my canal-side Cape Cod village. To me, these families are symbolic of what is being lost in most of America. They learned to cook, as my grandmother did, from their mothers and grand-mothers. They understood ingredients and technique as thoroughly as most highly trained chefs, but they never considered what they did day after day, week after week, season after season as out-of-the-ordinary. Most never wrote a recipe down. At best, they made a few notes in Italian or simply noted the ingredients without specific amounts. It was "a little of this" and "a pinch of that"—and the rest was left to intuition and instinct, both of which were nurtured as a matter of course during their childhoods at their mothers' sides.

My past is connected to my present with memories and symbols. I still have the brass corkscrew my grandfather used to open his homemade wine. I still have my grandmother's ravioli cutter. I have the hundred-year-old cheese knife from Louis's Market given to me by Jenny Bula, Louis's daughter, and my grandmother's Hoosier cabinet, still filled with the Old World memories. It is my lifetime connection to these people that I want to share with others in our culture who are looking for their roots. It is a slice of the past that is quickly becoming forgotten.

SWIFT & COMPANY

The Swift Family of Sagamore, "The Meat-Packing People" (Swift & Company), dates back almost to the beginning of Cape Cod and the town of West Sandwich, now Sagamore. Noble Swift (1830-1911) and his father William drove cattle, sheep, and hogs from the Brighton Market to Sagamore and Sandwich. There, the livestock was batched, dressed, and sold to dealers all over the Cape. Later Noble went into business with his two brothers, Gustavus and Nathan, and they began the now-famous Chicago plant with financing from Noble. Although Noble Swift had an interest in the Chicago operation, he maintained the family business on the Cape. He was also one of the early Bourne pioneers in cultivating cranberries on Cape Cod.

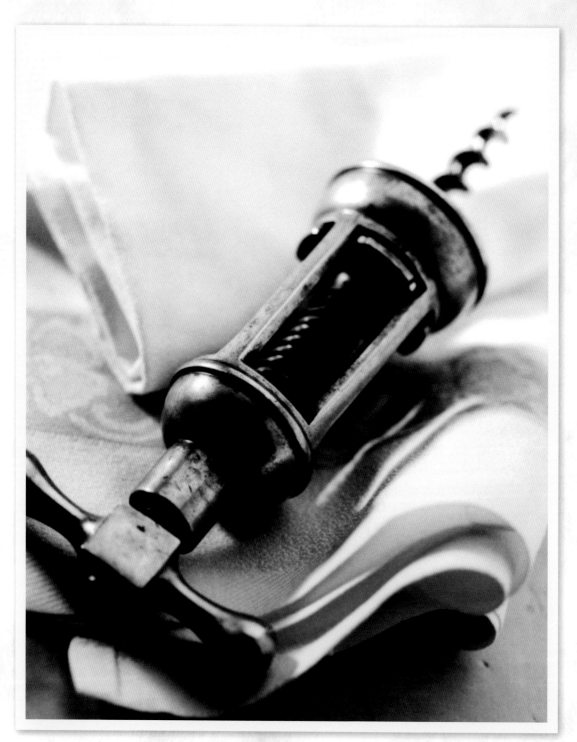

Grandfathers corkscrew he brought with him from Italy.

ANTIPASTI, APPETIZERS & SALADS

Antipasto

What better way to entertain guests for the holidays than with an *abbondanza* antipasto beautifully and artfully presented? It should be pretty to look at. Choose foods with lots of flavors and a variety of color and tastes. Usually this antipasto is not followed by a first course because it is very substantial. It is a dish meant to excite your guests, not to fill them. A good antipasto will create a spirit of conviviality, whether served before a meal or at a cocktail party.

Here is a list of suggestions:

Marinated mushrooms

Assortment of sliced meats: ruffles of prosciutto, salami and mortadella

Roasted red peppers

Fresh mozzarella balls

Chunks of Parmigiano Reggiano

Cubes of provolone cheese

Assortment of olives

Grape tomatoes

Toasted slices of small bread or bread sticks is a good accompaniment to the ingredients.

ASPARAGUS WRAPPED IN PROSCIUTTO

Here is asparagus in one of its most elegant guises: fresh stalks are cooked *al dente*, wrapped in thin slices of prosciutto, sprinkled with Parmigiano Reggiano, then placed under the broiler until cheese melts slightly and the asparagus is heated through.

SERVES 6 AS AN APPETIZER

18 large asparagus spears, trimmed

3 tablespoons butter

12 thin slices prosciutto di Parma

6 tablespoons grated Parmigiano Reggiano

Bring 1 to 2 cups of water to a boil in a frying pan large enough to hold the asparagus. Add the spears and cook *al dente*, being careful to not overcook.

Dry the asparagus with a dry towel.

Over high heat melt the butter in a saucepan large enough to hold all the asparagus. Once melted, add the dry spears and sauté, shaking the pan to coat the asparagus well. Set aside to cool.

Lay 2 slices of prosciutto, slightly overlapping, on a clean surface. Place 3 spears of asparagus (tips facing in the same direction) on one end of the prosciutto. Then roll the prosciutto around the asparagus with tips and ends showing and place on an oiled baking sheet. Repeat with remaining prosciutto and asparagus and top each with a tablespoon of Parmigiano Reggiano. At this point, if you're not ready to serve them, they may be refrigerated for an hour or two.

When ready to serve, place them under a broiler until heated through and the cheese melts.

ASPARAGUS WRAPPED IN PROSCIUTTO WITH FRESH MOZZARELLA

6 slices of prosciutto di
Parma, sliced thin

9 asparagus spears, with
2 inches cut off the stem
at the bottom

3 slices (½-inch thick round
slices) fresh mozzarella

2 tablespoons olive oil

Salt and pepper to taste

Balsamic glaze (either store-
bought or a house reduction
of balsamic vinegar)

Lay 2 slices of prosciutto side by side the long way on a work surface. Place 3 asparagus spears perpendicular to the prosciutto. Put 1 slice fresh mozzarella on top of the asparagus and wrap tightly with the prosciutto, securing the cheese.

Warm olive oil in a sauté pan over medium heat. Place the asparagus seam-side-down into the pan and cook until golden brown and slightly crispy. Repeat with the other side. Season with salt and pepper to taste.

Place cooked asparagus on a warm plate and drizzle with balsamic glaze.

CAMPO DI VINO

131 South Main St.
Barre, VT 05641
(802) 249-5543
campodivino.com

While in Barre, Vermont, I visited the family-run Campo di Vino and had the chance to meet Robert Campo Senior and his daughter-in-law Michele. I asked Bob about his history.

"My grandparents Giovanni and Maria came from Baveno, Piedmont, West of Lake Maggiore. I have lived my whole life in the house my grandfather bought back in 1903," he said.

Bob, now retired, worked for thirty-three years as a credit manager for Rock of Ages, a granite manufacturing company in Barre dating back to 1885. Michele told me she and her husband Bob Jr. opened Campo di Vino in 2008 because there was no good sausage available in Barre.

"We started with a secret family sausage recipe that was handed down to us by a few different people who owned the right to it," she said.

Along with that sausage, they now sell an assorted line of raviolis, some of the best I have had in a while. As I walked around the store, I noticed small preserved jars of antipasto. I asked Michele about the recipe and as she described the ingredients, I realized it was the antipasto Rose Sorenti, my surrogate mother, used to make.

I asked Bob if he had a favorite recipe he could share with me.

"I made this the other night," he explained. "Heat a tablespoon of olive oil in a fry pan, add a chopped-up onion, Luganega sausage that has been cut into bite-size pieces or a little larger if you like, diced potato, and a sliced sweet red pepper. Place a cover on the pan, turn heat to low, simmer until potatoes are done."

Sounds delicious. If you want to try it yourself and happen to be in the area, stop by and purchase some Luganega right from the source. It's a mild pork sausage sometimes sold by length and also sold by weight. The shop sells them in 5-inch lengths, about six to a package.

Beginning with a recipe that has been passed down over generations, Laura and Robert Campo, Sr., perfected theirs when it fell into their hands. It soon became a family delicacy, as only two batches were made a year, and they were reserved for special occasions and holidays. As others began to try it, and as the grandchildren fell in love with it, Laura and Robert, Sr., taught their sons the timely and involved process. Packed with mushrooms, olives, cauliflower, pickles, onions, and more, and slowly cooked in a unique and flavorful sauce, this antipasto is beyond compare.

This is the handwritten recipe for antipasto used by Rose Sorenti as well as Vino di Campo's recipe.

Drain all except oil in tuna & anchovies

Antipasto

this recipe's
13 pts
$5.00 1997

1 Cauliflower, cook in half water & half vinegar
salt to taste, do not over cook, remove from
water, in same water cook
3 red peppers do not overcook - drain and cool
add   2 cans mushrooms
2 cans Italian string beans   } Keep warn
2 jars onions   jars in oven
2 jars gherkins pickles   + rings
2   "   Artichokes   } Keep tops in hot
                                    water on stove,
2   "   Carrots   Bring water in blue
                                    canning pan to boil
2 cans Anchovies filet   place filled jars
                                    in a boil 20 min
2   "   "   capers
2 large cans tuna fish in olive oil
2 Green olives
2 black olives   Put one sardine in
   Parodi sardines   each jar, then close
2 Catsup   salt & pepper to taste
1 cup olive oil - 1 cup vinegar - let set
2 hrs. or more - then steam in jars 2 c min.

BAGNA CAUDA

Bagna cauda (pronounced BAHN-yah KOW-dah) is Italian for "hot bath," and is a savory dipping option that is quick and easy to prepare. Perfect as a chic finger food for your next cocktail party or at a casual dinner for friends and family, bagna cauda can be served right in the same dish or pot in which it is made.

MAKES ABOUT 1½ CUPS

1 cup extra-virgin olive oil

3 tablespoons unsalted butter

1 tablespoon garlic, finely minced

1 (2-ounce) can rolled anchovy fillets with capers

¼ cup finely chopped fresh Italian parsley

Combine the olive oil, butter, and garlic in a chafing dish, cast-iron pan, or enamel or earthenware casserole. Simmer for a few minutes over medium heat, being careful to not let the garlic turn brown.

Add the anchovies with the capers and the parsley. Simmer the mixture for 15 minutes, or until the flavors are well integrated. (The anchovies will dissolve.) Remove the pot from the stove and place it over a candle warmer or spirit lamp. Serve it with assorted crisp vegetables and Italian or French bread. A bold, spirited red wine such as a Valpolicella makes a wonderful accompaniment, or, if you prefer white, choose a crisp Soave.

BAGNET

Bagnet hails from the Piedmont region of Italy, and was brought here by immigrants who came to work in the garnet sheds of Barre, Vermont. It is perfect spread on toast points or as a spread on watery vegetables such as cabbage or endive.

MAKES ABOUT 5½ CUPS

2–3 cups chopped fresh Italian parsley

3 cloves garlic, chopped

2 red or green peppers, cut into large pieces

1 large carrot, cut into large pieces

2 medium onions, cut into large pieces

1 cup olive oil

2 (2-ounce) cans anchovies (with or without capers)

2 (8-ounce) cans tomato sauce

¼ cup vinegar, or to taste

¼ teaspoon red pepper flakes, or to taste

Put parsley, garlic, peppers, carrot, and onions through a meat grinder, alternating small amounts of each ingredient as you proceed. Set aside.

In a medium saucepan, heat the oil and anchovies, dissolving the anchovies completely. To the oil and anchovies, add the vegetable mixture, tomato sauce, vinegar, and red pepper flakes. Bring to a boil and cook uncovered over medium-low heat for 20 to 30 minutes, stirring frequently. This recipe can then be stored in the refrigerator for up to two weeks. It also freezes well for up to three months.

GLOUCESTER FISHERMEN'S WIVES CALAMARI TRIZZANO

This recipe is from The *Gloucester Fishermen's Wives Cookbook,* a dish from Angela Sanfilippo, who has been president of the Wives since 1977.

SERVES 5-6

⅓ cup olive oil

2 cups onions, sliced

3 pounds fresh calamari, cleaned and cut into rings

3 tablespoons pine nuts

3 tablespoons raisins

¼ cup chopped fresh Italian parsley 2 teaspoons salt

Black pepper to taste

1 (28-ounce) can crushed tomatoes

1 pound spaghetti (optional)

Grated Romano cheeese, to taste

Heat oil in a skillet and sauté onions. Add calamari and sauté until golden brown.

Add nuts, raisins, parsley, salt, pepper, and crushed tomatoes. Cook at medium heat for about 20 minutes. Remove from heat and let sit for 15 minutes.

Serve in individual bowls with Italian bread.

When serving with spaghetti, cook spaghetti according to package directions. Drain and mix with calamari sauce. Sprinkle with Romano cheese. Can also be served over white rice.

LURGIO IMPORTS

134 Preservation Way
Wakefield, RI 02879
(401) 783-2387
www.dellortooil.com

As I began my interview with Dennis Lurgio of Dell'Orto Olive, I became more fascinated in how he discovered his roots than in his exquisite and delicious olive oil.

In 1999, Dennis's uncle gave him a marriage license and documentation of his grandparents' wedding day. "I was interested in genealogy at the time," he explains. "I went to a genealogy website and typed in "Lurgio," and up came names of Lurgios in the small village of Oliveto Citra, Campania, Italy. I did not know if we were related or not. I made a few calls to people in the village. Many did not know what I was talking about because they did not speak English and I did not speak Italian. I finally reached a 30-year-old woman, Teresa Lurgio, who was not comfortable talking on the phone and told me to take a bus to the village, not knowing I was in the United States."

Dennis and Teresa agreed to write to each other. "She sent me photos and post cards of her family and said, "All the Lurgio's in Oliveto Citra are all related." Eventually Dennis was invited to visit Teresa and her family. Three months later he was on a plane to Campania, Italy. When he arrived he spent two days in the local church going through records, some dating back to the sixteenth century. Here was his ancestors' and heritage. "I had hit the genealogy lottery," he explained. "It was incredible, a very emotional time and the best experience I think I have ever had."

It was on this trip he learned about the Dell'Orto olive groves with their 2,000 trees dating back to the 1850s. He started to order the olive oil to give as gifts. Then, in 2005, he had the idea of expanding his gift-giving hobby into an official business.

Lurgio's olive oil is DOP certified by the EU. He has won many competitions, including receiving "The Best Olive Oils of the World" in the New York International Olive Oil Competition in 2014.

Extra
Virgin
Olive Oil

Oleificio
Dell'Orto
Oliveto Citra
1870

Superior
Quality

First Cold
Press
Product of Italy
All Natural
No Preservatives
25.36 FL.oz
0.75 ℓ e

Extra
Virgin
Olive Oil

GOLD

NEW YORK
INTERNATIONAL
OLIVE OIL
COMPETITION

SILVER 2013

Los Angeles International
Olive Oil
Competition
2013

Oleificio
Dell'Orto
Oliveto Citra
1870

100%
ORGANIC

Product
of Italy

USDA
ORGANIC

First Cold Press
All Natural
No Preservatives

16.91 FL.oz

Extra
Virgin
Olive Oil

SILVER

LOS ANGELES
International

Oleificio
Dell'Orto
Oliveto Citra
1870

D.O.P.
Protected Designation of Origin
"COLLINE SALERNITANE"

First Cold
Press
Product of Italy
All Natural
No Preservatives

CANNELLINI BEAN DIP

Here is a fast and easy dip for your next gathering. Serve it in a bowl surrounded by cut up vegetables for a party appetizer. For lunch, spread it on warm pita bread pockets with lettuce and tomato slices. For a Mexican twist, use ½ cup fresh cilantro leaves, a small jalapeño pepper in lieu of the the sage or basil, and serve it with fried tortilla chips instead of the sage or basil. Instead of a bowl, you can also serve this dip in large pieces of fennel as shown here.

MAKES ABOUT 2 CUPS

1–2 cloves garlic

2–6 fresh sage or basil leaves

1 (19-ounce) can cannellini (white kidney) beans, rinsed and drained.

¼ cup good, high-quality olive oil

Freshly ground pepper and salt to taste

Assorted fresh vegetables for dipping: broccoli florets (blanched); carrot sticks; red, yellow, or green peppers, cut into strips; and fennel.

In a food processor fitted with a steel blade, process the garlic and sage or basil for 3 seconds. Add the cannelloni beans and process until smooth. With the machine still running, add the olive oil. Turn machine off, add pepper and salt and process for 1 minute. If mixture is too thick, add 2 to 3 teaspoons water. Place mixture in a colorful bowl and drizzle with a good olive oil. If you like, garnish with a sprinkling of chopped tomato and a sprig of sage or basil (or, if going Mexican, a few cilantro leaves).

Cannellini Beans and Bread
"Every Saturday, when my mother was working, my father would make his favorite meal. He would soak the beans the night before, cook them the next day, and toss them together in olive oil with pieces of dried, stale bread, salt, and pepper."

—*Dennis Lurgio*

BOSTON'S LITTLE ITALY

In the North End of Boston's Little Italy are several businesses owned by first-, second-, and third-generation immigrants, but there is also a new generation of owners who have taken over older establishments. The North End is now adapting to a different clientele while trying to hold on to tradition.

A small number of Italian immigrants first came to the North End around 1860 from Genoa, making their living as fruit and vegetable vendors and peddling cheeses, wine, and fresh breads. During the 1880s Irish immigrants started to populate the area and began to relocate to other neighborhoods. Most of these later Italian immigrants came from Campania and Sicily. They colonized the wharf area along the harbor around 1925 and worked on the profitable commercial fishing fleets. Later, other Italians from Avellino, Naples, and Abruzzo arrived, finding work as masons, metalworkers, carpenters, and laborers.

It was here, in the North End, that three Sicilian friends founded the Prince Pasta Company in 1912. Prince started as a small spaghetti manufacturing company at 92 Prince Street. The company outgrew its offices and, in 1941, moved to Lowell, Massachusetts. A fourth Sicilian, Guiseppe Pellegrino, eventually took over the company and it remained in his family until 1987.

Another famous business was also established in the North End, Pastene Products. Luigi Pastene started selling produce from a pushcart in 1848. Around 1874, he founded Pastene Products and was later joined by his son Pietro, and together they built the company into a specialty Italian import grocery. Today Pastene Corporation distributes its products throughout the United States as well as Italy.

In 1920, outside of Boston in Braintree, Massachusetts, two Italian-born anarchists, Nicola Sacco and Bartolomeo Vanzetti, were wrongfully convicted of murdering a guard and paymaster during an armed robbery of a shoe factory. They then found themselves at the center of one of the largest causes in modern history. In 1927, large protests were held around the world with famous writers and artists pleading for their innocence. The governor appointed a commission to investigate the case, but the commission upheld the verdict and the two men were executed on August 23, 1927. Many concluded after their deaths that the pair was convicted because of anti-Italian prejudice and their anarchist political beliefs and that they were unjustly executed. Fifty years later, in 1977, Massachusetts Governor Michael Dukakis issued a proclamation stating, "Any disgrace should be forever removed from their names." He did not, however, proclaim Sacco and Vanzetti innocent.

V. CIRCACE & SON, INC.

173 North St.
Boston, MA 02109
(617) 227-3193
vcirace.com

When Prohibition ended on December 5, 1933, V. Cirace & Son in Boston's North End was granted the first license to sell liquor in the City of Boston.

Founded in 1906 by Ernesto and Vincenza Cirace, immigrants from Salerno, the business was originally a wholesale purveyor of groceries, dry goods, and tobacco. After World War II, Ernest, a Suffolk Law graduate, and his sister Eda—the next generation—joined the business and focused on growing the wine and spirits venture. Today, Ernest's children, Jeffrey Cirace and his sister Lisa, run the business.

"My father and his sister were partners, so now my sister and I are partners," says Jeff.

This is a company that believes in tradition. Jeff, who has worked at Cirace for 46 years, told me the outside of the brick building with its large display windows looks much as it did in the 1940s. Inside the store, the counter, shelving, and hardwood floor are original.

"The center of the store and the back of the store were warehouse space," Jeff said. "Then when I came into the business, I started expanding, changing that warehouse space to retail."

The store now stocks wines from all over the world, but specializes in wine from Italy and California. It also has a large selection of other alchoholic beverages.

"Our grappa selection has been selected a couple of times as the biggest grappa selection in the United States," Jeff added. "We focus our attention on Italian spirits, Italian Amaros, rare bourbons. We try to differentiate ourselves from other retailers by offering a selection that you wouldn't normally find anywhere else. That's what sets us apart from other wine and spirit shops in the city and the state."

The store's staff has educated itself on fine spirits and grappa. "Customers can come in here and ask for suggestions on wines to complement their menu or what they're serving for dinner one night," Jeff said. "You won't wander around in here. I want my staff to engage with people. We have a lot of regular clients who have been coming in the shop for a long, long time and that's what I try to base our business on."

As well as wine and spirits, the store sells imported olive oils and beautiful gift baskets featuring pasta, salami, *biscotti*, oil, and other regional Italian specialties.

CAPRI COSMOPOLITAN

This recipe may be doubled or tripled.

MAKES 1 COCKTAIL

1 ounce vodka

1 ounce cranberry juice

½ ounce limoncello

Lemon peel or sliced cranberries for garnish

In a shaker with ice, combine vodka, cranberry juice, and limoncello. Shake slightly and strain into a martini glass, garnish with a lemon peel or sliced cranberries for color.

THE ITALIAN KITCHEN

91 Common St.
Lawrence, MA 01840
(978) 685-1652

Peter Messina of the Italian Kitchen was born in 1944 in the small town of Via-grande in the province of Catania, on the east coast of Italy near the volcano, Mount Etna and came to the United States in 1955 with his brother and father and settled in the Massachusetts mill town of Lawrence with the rest of the family. In 1958 Peter's father and a few friends started a small storefront called The Italian Kitchen. They specialized in making Sicilian *crespelle* and rice balls (*arancini*), a tradition that started when the men made them for the Feast of the Three Saints, a three-day festival occurring every Labor Day weekend. Peter, 13 at the time, worked with his father and was taught the techniques it takes to make these savory and sweet fried dough treats. After the festival, the men realized the popularity of this Sicilian food.

They all had regular day jobs, but continued making and selling their *crespelle* on the weekends as a way to make extra money and connect to their Italian roots. Peter carries on the tradition to this day, running The Italian Kitchen, which now specializes in catering and offers a variety of delectable Italian cuisine, including three versions of *crespelle*: the first is plain in the shape of round balls and sprinkled with powdered sugar, a second has the dough wrapped around anchovies, and a third is stuffed with ricotta cheese. All are delicious.

CRESPELLE

Crespelle are a unique treat born in Sicily in the 1930s. They are somewhat different than Neapolitan Zeppoli in taste and texture and have a different history. After finishing baking bread, in an environment where refrigeration was unavailable, Sicilian women would take the leftover dough and make a snack food. They would wrap an anchovy in the dough and then deep-fry it, making a *crespelle*. Sometimes they would substitute ricotta cheese for the anchovy.

Chef Peter A. Messina in Lawrence, Massachussettes, says that many people have tried to replicate the taste of his *crespelle*, or, as he spells it, "crispellis", but it's tough. One important technique is mixing the dough by hand to get the right consistency, it cannot be done by machine. Peter says it's all in the feel. Peter would not reveal his secret dough recipe for his famous crispellis, but the Basic Pizza Napoletana Dough recipe on page 73 works well.

MAKES 1–2 DOZEN

Your favorite pizza dough, prepared according to recipe directions

Oil for frying

FOR PLAIN *CRESPELLE*:
Sugar for dusting

FOR ANCHOVY *CRESPELLE*:
12 to 24 anchovies

FOR RICOTTA *CRESPELLE*:
I tablespoon for each

For plain *crespelle*, scoop pinball-sized dollops of dough into hot oil in a heavy skillet and fry until golden. Transfer to paper towel and dust with sugar.

To make anchovy *crespelle*, take a piece of dough and create an indentation. Place 1 or 2 anchovies in the middle and wrap them with the dough to form a ball. Flour hands first—it will make it easier to handle the dough. Place balls into hot oil and fry until golden. Transfer to paper towel to drain.

To make ricotta *crespelle*, follow the same procedure as for the anchovy, but place a tablespoon of ricotta into each of the indentations.

BRICCO'S

141 Hanover St., Boston MA, (617) 248-6800, bricco.com

Behind 241 Hanover Street is 11 Broad Alley, which leads to Bricco Panetteria (617-248-9859, bricco.com/panetteria), one of the best artisanal bread bakeries in the Boston area, and Bricco Salumeria and Pasta Shop (617-248-9629, bricco-salumeria.com), where you can buy Italian sliced meats, fresh pasta, olives, and the best mozzarella, made daily by store manager Gussippi Locilento.

FORMAGGIO KITCHEN SOUTH END

268 Shawmut Ave., Boston, MA 02118, (617) 350-6996

formaggiokitchen.com

The Formaggio Kitchen began in 1978, starting with a location in Cambridge, Massachusetts. They had one vision, to create a European shopping experience. Today, they have three locations: Boston, Cambridge, and New York that all offer broad and unusual selections of cheese. While Formaggio Kitchen is best known for their cheeses, they offer so much more. They travel throughout the United States and Europe to find the freshest ingredients. They sell charcuterie, sweets, rare spices, pantry staples, natural wines, craft beers, and freshly baked breads from local bakeries. The staff at Formaggio Kitchen are more than happy to help you find the best wine to go with whichever cheese you pick. They also have their in-house chefs create an assortment of fresh seasonal sides and salads to include alongside their deli products.

ITALIA UNITA

Lisa Cappuccio lives in East Boston, Massachusetts, and is president of Italia Unita, which promotes Italian culture and heritage. She is also the marketing coordinator for *Bostoniano Magazine* and author of *Vino e Pomodori Tradizioni Italiane.* Lisa grew up in East Boston with her parents, Vincenzo and Lina Capogreco, who both came from Calabria, Italy. Despite the urban setting, Vincenzo has always produced a high percentage of the family's food, everything from home-grown vegetables to wine. "Everything is really like from farm to table, but we live in the city," says Lisa. "This whole organic movement—my father's been doing that since he was a kid and never stopped."

When the Capogrecos settled in East Boston in about 1960, Vincenzo opened a deli/produce/pasta store called Bennington Food Market at 32 Bennington Street in East Boston. He ran the store for about 35 years, and still sells starter plants, produce, and flowers. In the early days, Lisa said, East Boston was about 90 percent Italian. In the streets she would hear the spoken dialects of various parts of Southern Italy such as Avellino and Naples as well as Sicily. Lisa's household remained very traditional, and very Calabrian. Lina's cooking was never "watered down" by the prevalent Italian-American cuisine.

"My parents cooked homemade all the time," she recalled. "We didn't grow up going out to dinner." Except for an occasional

Saturday night pizza, "my mother cooked every night. My father worked, and everything was homemade."

The family's diet remained Calabrese, and they ate lots of pasta, beans, eggplant, and pork. In the summer the extended family and friends preserved tomatoes—200 or 300 Mason jars worth.

"Even though it's East Boston," Lisa says of her father, "he has a really, really big garden. Vincenzo grows beans, eggplant, and zucchini. "And," Lisa says, "he grows things like the Sicilian squash, which can grow up to 10 feet."

The zucchini produce blossoms that are a staple of every dinner in the summer. As for the varieties of beans he can't grow, he buys them at the grocery store. Her mother shells them and freezes them, and the family eats fresh frozen beans all winter.

Lisa's mother made her own ricotta, substituting fig leaves for rennet. Lisa explains that the the sap of the juice from the fig leaf was what made the ricotta. Where was the fig tree? Growing in the back yard, of course.

Vincenzo also made his own wine.

And then there's the pig.

One day when Lisa was about 12, she walked into the family's apartment with her friends. "There was a pig, a dead pig, on our table. I was like, 'Oh my God,' and my friends were like, 'What's that?'"

Of course, you're embarrassed as a kid. I couldn't believe they didn't warn me!"

Do you remember the old advertising slogan "Wednesday is Prince Spaghetti Day?" Lisa's family, like the Italian families of Boston's North End in the advertisement, ate according to a weekly schedule. Monday was soup and Tuesday was either pasta or meat, such as a roast, or both. Wednesday was *pastasciutta*, which was spaghetti with tomato sauce. Thursday was beans. Friday, as in many Catholic cities, was fish. Saturday was steak, and Sunday "was always the traditional Italian dinner, meatballs and pasta and chicken cutlets, veal cutlets, everything," Lisa said.

STUFFED EGGPLANT

The following recipe from the Cappuccio kitchen is not precise, says Lisa. "My mother never used a recipe. She simply threw in a 'little this and a little that.' Stuffed eggplants were a staple at my home every Sunday dinner."

YIELD: 8 STUFFED EGGPLANTS

2 medium eggplants

1 cup Pecorino Romano cheese

1½ cup grated bread crumbs

4 cloves garlic, sliced very small

Bunch of basil, cut up very small

1 egg (plus 1 egg white)

Dash of salt

⅓ cup vegetable oil for frying

Grated cheese for topping

Cut the eggplant in half, down the length. Place in boiling water for about 25 to 30 minutes. Strain and let cool.

Once cooled, spoon out the flesh from the peel, reserving the peels. Cut flesh into small pieces and place in a large bowl. Add cheese, bread crumbs, garlic, basil, egg and salt, and mix all together.

With a large spoon, stuff the reserved eggplant peels with the mixture, being careful to not overstuff. Baste the top with a little egg white. Continue with the rest of the peels.

Preheat a frying pan with oil on medium heat. Place the eggplant (stuffing facing down) in the frying pan. Let it cook on the stuffing side for about 5 minutes, then turn over for another
4 minutes.

Place cooked eggplant on paper towels to drain.

Serve on a platter with grated cheese sprinkled on top.

NORTH END MARKET TOURS

50 Charter St.
Boston, MA 02113
bostonfoodtours.com

Michele Topor is the ambassadress of Boston's Little Italy in the North End. I met Michele when we were both students studying for our chef's diplomas at Madeleine Kamman's Modern Gourmet in Newton, Massachusetts. At the time, we all had day jobs—Michele was a nurse, and I worked as a designer for a large publishing company. We worked hard, our classes started at 5 p.m. and sometimes went until 11 p.m., four nights a week. When our class graduated we all made different career changes. Michele, with her love of food and Italian culture, found herself gravitating to Boston's Little Italy, where she bought a small building and started teaching cooking classes and catering from her home. During this time Michele took frequent trips to Italy, immersing herself in the food and culture. She went back several times, studying with Marcella Hazan in Bologna at La Scuola Di Cucina, and again with Giuliano Bugialli in Florence.

Her love and passion for Italian food and culture led Michele to design North End Market Tours. Since 1994, she and her personally trained guides have shared their passion for food and their knowledge of history to guide participants through the North End's specialty shops, tasting foods along the way.

Her cooking classes, market tours, and culinary trips to Italy have been featured on the Travel Channel, TV Food Network, HGTV, and CNN. Michele has become one of Boston's leading authorities on Italian food, wine, and culture.

I had not seen Michele for several years when we reconnected. We sat at her kitchen table over a cup of tea reminiscing about our past lives. I also had the opportunity to see her award-winning rooftop garden with it's beautiful fig and lemon trees and large variety of herbs in huge pots.

INSALATA DI ARANCIE (SALAD WITH ORANGES)

"Sicily has an overabundance of oranges in many varieties. In the winter and spring season, the famous blood oranges can be found. Sliced oranges make a terrific palate cleanser and are often found paired with fish." —Michele Topor

SERVES 4-6

6 oranges, peeled with the white pith removed

1 red onion, thinly sliced and soaked in water for at least 30 minutes

3 tablespoons olive oil

1 tablespoon red wine vinegar

Salt and fresh ground pepper to taste

Several oil-cured olives

Chopped fresh Italian parsley for garnish

Fennel, thinly sliced

Cut the oranges into segments (see photo) and place in a shallow salad bowl.

Drain the onions and pat dry.

Dress the oranges with the onion, olive oil, and vinegar. Season to taste with salt and pepper.

Garnish with olives, parsley, and fennel.

This salad is best if allowed to marinate for 30 minutes before serving.

ALBA PRODUCE

8 Parmenter St.
Boston, MA 02113

How's this for a business model? Don't hang a sign outside your retail establishment. For Bruce Alba, the owner of a North End *fruttivendo* (Italian for a place to buy fruit and vegetables), it works just fine.

Everybody calls Bruce "Albie" or, alternatively, "the vegetable guy." Albie went to work here in the 1980s with his neighbor Rosario Mogoverro, a Sicilian who ran this place for 35 or 40 years. "We lived right across the street from each other, so I used to just help him," he says.

Albie was a student then, and he'd wake at 4 a.m., go down to the Chelsea Market to help Rosario buy the produce and load his van, and then they'd set everything up in the store. "By 7:30 or 8:00 a.m., I would get out of here," Albie said. "I did that for eight years."

When Rosario retired in 1994, Albie took over the store and kept everything the same. He is known for his California olives which, when they arrive, are rock

hard. Albie first pits the olives, then soaks them for two weeks in a water and salt solution, which he changes every two or three days. At that point, if the olive has lost its bitterness, it is ready to be flavored. Albie's favorite flavorings are garlic, peppers, fennel, fennel seed, oil, vinegar, and thyme.

Along with fresh produce, Albie also sells pasta and a selection of canned goods. The store is tucked into a non-descript spot next to an Italian restaurant. Albie's customers, who remain unsure of the exact name of the store, say Albie not only has the freshest produce at the best prices, he is also very, very friendly. Sign or no, they know where to find Albie.

ALBIE'S OLIVE SCHIACCIATE

MAKES 2 POUNDS

2 pounds green unripe olives, with pits

½ cup salt

Several garlic cloves

Several sprigs of fresh thyme

2–3 tablespoons fennel seed, chili pepper, or your choice of seasonings

Olive oil

Crush the olives with a hammer or meat tenderizer, to remove the pits. This will allow greater penetration of the brine into the olives and they will be ready to eat in a shorter time. Discard the pits.

Put the olives in a large bowl and cover with water and a handful of salt. Keep in a cool area, changing the salted water every day until most of the bitterness of the olives has been removed. The olives should retain some crunch. The process could take from 4 days to 2 weeks.

When olives are ready, rinse them well, drain, and put in a jar with garlic, thyme, and fennel seeds (or your choice of flavorings). Cover with olive oil. They will be ready to eat in a couple of days, but will keep for 2 to 3 months refrigerated.

ALBIE'S SPECIAL VINEGAR PEPPERS

MAKES 1 QUART

6–8 St. Nicholas/Christmas peppers (or other medium-size flat, green and red pepper)

2–3 garlic cloves, crushed

Pinch of salt

2 sprigs fresh thyme

2 celery stocks, chopped

Red or white wine vinegar or distilled white vinegar

Thoroughly wash peppers, keep whole or slice. Place in a large jar with garlic, salt, thyme and sliced celery. Fill the jar to ¾ full with vinegar and top off with water and cover with a lid.

Keep in a cool place for about 1 month. Check every 2 days to be sure the peppers are always covered with liquid, adding more if necessary.

ALBIE'S MARINATED OLIVES

MAKES ABOUT 2 QUARTS

4 cups mixed olives of your choice

1 tablespoon fresh thyme leaves

5 or 6 fresh rosemary leaves

2 tablespoons fresh lemon juice

4 cloves garlic, peeled and thinly sliced

¼ cup extra-virgin oil

8–10 black peppercorns

Combine all ingredients in a medium bowl, mix well, cover, and refrigerate for 1 to 2 days, stirring occasionally.

ALBIE'S MARINATED MUSHROOMS

MAKES 1–2 PINTS

½ cup extra-virgin olive oil

2 pounds assorted mushrooms, cleaned and quartered

2 lemons, zested and juiced

3 garlic cloves, sliced

Several sprigs fresh thyme

2 bay leaves

Kosher salt and freshly ground black pepper to taste

Add ¼ cup olive oil to a large skillet over medium heat. Add the mushrooms and cook for 2 to 3 minutes. Remove from the heat and stir in the lemon zest and juice, garlic, thyme, and bay leaves. Pour in remaining olive oil and season the mixture with salt and pepper. Pour into a bowl and allow to cool.

Pour into a small jar with a cover and refrigerate until ready to serve.

Serve at room temperature.

STUFFED ARTICHOKES

This recipe is great to make in the spring when artichokes are in season.

SERVES 4 AS AN APPETIZER.

4 fresh medium-size artichokes

1½ cups water

1 teaspoon salt

Juice of ½ lemon

2 cloves garlic, minced

3 tablespoons minced fresh Italian parsley

1 teaspoon fresh oregano

1 teaspoon fresh thyme

1 teaspoon fresh basil

1 cup dried breadcrumbs

¼ cup Parmigiano Reggiano cheese

¼ cup olive oil, plus more for drizzling

Salt and freshly ground pepper to taste

½ cup dry white wine

Melted butter for dipping

Trim the prickly end of the leaves with kitchen scissors and cut bottoms so they stand up. Place the four artichokes in a saucepan with ½ cup water, salt, and lemon juice. Cover and cook on high heat for 15 to 20 minutes. Remove from pan and let cool.

In a medium bowl combine the garlic, herbs, breadcrumbs, cheese, and olive oil and mix well. Add salt and pepper to taste.

Open each artichoke by spreading out the leaves. Spoon the stuffing in and around the leaves, using about ¼ cup of stuffing for each artichoke.

Preheat the oven to 350°F.

Place the artichokes in an ovenproof casserole. Add the white wine and remaining 1 cup water. Drizzle each artichoke with a little more olive oil, cover with aluminum foil, and bake for 1 hour.

Serve with melted butter for dipping.

Iron cookware that belonged to my grandmother and aunt.

SAUCES

ANCHOVY SAUCE

A tasty twist on an old classic. The difference is that you partially cook the pasta, then finish cooking it in the sauce over high heat, making a very rich and intense dish. Don't worry about the amount of pasta water you're adding to the sauce. It will reduce as it cooks and helps bind the sauce.

SERVES 4

¼ cup olive oil

1 (2-ounce) can anchovies packed in olive oil, undrained

1–3 garlic cloves, finely chopped

¼ teaspoon red pepper flakes

2 tablespoons tomato paste

½ cup dry white wine

3 tablespoons drained capers in brine (or capers in salt, rinsed and drained)

½ heaping cup chopped fresh Italian parsley

Zest of 1 lemon, grated

Salt (for cooking linguine)

1 pound linguine

Heat olive oil over medium heat in a deep, heavy skillet large enough to hold the cooked pasta (about 12 inches in diameter).

Add the anchovies, garlic, and red pepper and sauté gently, stirring often, until the garlic turns golden. Immediately dissolve the tomato paste in the wine and stir into the mixture. Stir in the capers and about ⅓ cup of the parsley, reserving the rest.

Reduce the heat to low and simmer the sauce, uncovered, for 10 to 15 minutes.

Meanwhile, bring 5 quarts water to a boil in a large (6- to 8-quart) saucepan. Add the lemon zest while it heats. When the water boils, add the salt, drop in the linguini, and cook just until it has wilted, about 1 minute. It will still be close to raw.

Add 3 to 4 ladlefuls of the linguine cooking water to the anchovy sauce. Drain the linguine in a colander and add it to the sauce in the skillet, toss or stir with two wooden spoons or a pasta fork to distribute the contents. Turn the heat to high and finish cooking the pasta in the sauce, uncovered, for about 8 minutes. The liquid will reduce and the pasta will be *al dente*.

To serve, turn into four large heated bowls and sprinkle with the reserved chopped parsley.

FIFTEEN-MINUTE FRESH TOMATO SAUCE

This sauce is a must-have recipe for a quick tasty and delicious sauce for any pasta. It is also perfect for serving over fish.

MAKES ABOUT 4 CUPS

2–3 tablespoons olive oil

2 cloves garlic, minced

1 small hot pepper or a few shakes red pepper flakes (optional)

12 large ripe tomatoes, blanched, skin removed, seeded and coarsely chopped

3 tablespoons chopped fresh Italian parsley

1 tablespoon chopped fresh marjoram

3 tablespoons chopped fresh basil

½ teaspoon chopped fresh thyme

Salt and freshly ground pepper to taste

Heat olive oil in a medium saucepan over medium heat. Add garlic and pepper (if using). Cook for 3 minutes until the garlic starts to turn light brown.

Add all the remaining ingredients, stir, and bring to a boil. Turn down the heat and simmer the sauce for 15 minutes, stirring occasionally. This sauce can be used immediately, stored in the refrigerator for a few days, or frozen for further use.

DIFIORE RAVIOLI SHOP

556 Franklin Ave., Hartford, CT 06114, (860) 296-1077
difioreraviolishop.com

Before researching this book, the only thing I knew about Hartford, Connecticut, was that Franklin Avenue is Hartford's Italian section. Like so many of my adventures with this project, I was pleasantly surprised at what I learned.

As I drove up Franklin Avenue, I spotted a store with a bright, colorful sign set back from the street. A small car with a logo advertising the DiFore Ravioli Shop was parked in front of the shop. I parked, walked in, and looked around the friendly room at the overwhelming varieties of homemade pastas: farfalle, rigatoni, spaghetti, fusilli, and many more. The store also stocks ravioli stuffed with lobster, walnut and gorgonzola, eggplant and mozzarella. Don't forget the homemade preserved sauces to go with the pastas: traditional marinara, chunky pomodoro, arrabbiata, and Bolognese to name a few. Several of the shelves house imported olive oils and many familiar Italian products. An old pasta machine sits high on a shelf. I asked the woman at the cash register if I could speak to the owner. A minute later two gentlemen came out of the backroom and introduced themselves.

"My name is Don and this is my son Daniel. I am second generation and Daniel's third," Don said. "My father Andy and mom Louise DiFiore started this business 32 years ago." Don's father, Andy DiFiore's parents, came from outside of Palermo, Sicily, and his mother was a farm girl from Wisconsin. But the predominant food flavors in their household came from his father's Sicilian and southern Italian background.

"My father was in the corporate sales and marketing world in New York City," Don explained, "but always loved good food. He was a foodie before the term was popular." Andy DiFiore always wanted to be in the restaurant and food world. At 62, as retirement age approached, he left the corporate world and decided to open a pasta shop.

"I am 57," said Don, "and cannot imagine five years from now changing careers and opening another business."

Andy opened his pasta shop in another location and subsequently shared a building with Don's restaurant, DiFiore Ristorante, which Don operated for 10 years. When the pasta shop needed more space 17 years ago, Andy moved to this location on Franklin Street, where it is now a landmark in Hartford's Little Italy.

A few years ago, when Andy passed away, Don's mother wanted to close the shop. Don wouldn't hear of it.

"I had been in the restaurant business over the years and Daniel is an aspiring chef, so we decided to carry on the family tradition together," Don said. "It was perfect timing."

I asked if I could tour the kitchen where the sauces and pasta are made. Both father and son proudly escorted me into the back. When he took over the business, Don upgraded the property by putting in a new kitchen, reworking the front of the store

with new cases, and making the shop more appealing. Business is up 100 percent in the last three years, Don said. In fact, in 2014 DiFiore Ravioli Shop was voted Connecticut's Favorite Small Business.

Despite the renovations, one thing did not change—the vintage pasta-making machines and equipment, which are 50 or 60 years old. "They don't make them like this anymore," Don said. "They run flawlessly and I would not replace them for new equipment for anything." I turned and looked at the extrusion machine, a large workhorse that extrudes all shapes of pasta. This is truly old world, a lost tradition carried on by two compassionate men.

The DiFiores supply many of the stores and restaurants in the area with their pastas and sauces. If you cannot get to Hartford and choose to make your own favorite sauce, Don and Daniel have many suggestions on their website of ways to combine the pasta with the right sauce.

MAMA GALLONI'S AUTHENTIC GOURMET FOODS & COOKING SCHOOL

1325 Springfield St., Suite 5
Feeding Hills, MA 01030
(413) 372-4305
mamagalloni.com

"There's nothing better than the smell of homemade pasta," says Betty Couture Magalony. "Once you eat it, you never go back."

And she should know. Betty is an aficionado of homemade pasta, and a teacher of traditional Italian food preparation. She makes pasta such as tortellini, ravioli, and gnocchi—from scratch—and for a decade she ran pasta-making classes from her house. When she decided the house had gotten too small for her class of 12, she opened her shop in Feeding Hills. Here she offers gourmet foods to go as well as classes.

"I enjoy it, enjoy cooking, bringing people in, showing them the real way to make pasta," she said. "The real way."

"[Students] come in and they'll cry, they'll smile, say 'my mom used to do this, but I never learned. My aunt, my mother—I never paid attention. Now they want to learn," Betty said.

While Betty's father Gavino Galloni came from northern Italy, her mother Lizzy came from a mountain town that was destroyed in a mudslide. Both parents immigrated to America when they were six, and met here. They raised seven children, five of them girls, in West Springfield. Betty was the youngest, and learned to cook authentic Italian food at her mother's knee. She's happy to now pass that knowledge along to others.

The two-hour pasta-making classes run for four weeks in the evening. Betty's students make white, whole wheat, and spinach pasta, ravioli, tortellini, and gnocchi. The class also cooks gourmet sauces to go with the pasta dishes, and finishes the evening by eating dinner. Students take home the leftovers. In a separate one-evening session, students can learn to make only sauces. On another evening Betty demonstrates how to make authentic stuffed *braciole* in her homemade red sauce. She also offers a gnocchi class for children ages 10 and older. And then there are "date nights"—two-hour sessions for a small group of couples who want not only a gourmet four-course dinner, but a cooking lesson as well.

Betty's daughter, son, daughter-in-law, and four grandchildren assist her in the business. The youngest ones wash dishes in the kitchen while Betty's daughter-in-law runs the front. Her son and daughter run the back. Betty teaches the classes and makes salads and the food for sale in the gleaming display cases. Mama Galloni's caters events and offers gourmet meals for four that are prepared to order. Her menu includes delicious desserts, such as traditional cannoli and classic *brasadella* filled with raspberry or lemon.

One of the aspects of her work that Betty loves is keeping the old traditions alive. "Let me get my hands in the pasta and cut that pasta," she says. "Today everything is so fast, family is not family." Back when Betty grew up, the whole family came home for supper every evening, and Sunday dinner was a big event. Her mother, Mama Galloni, "made soup-to-pasta all the time," Betty said. "I never knew there was boxed pasta until I was about six or seven years old. It was no good in the box. She made it; it was a way of life for us."

Betty feels her late mother would be proud to walk in to the business that bears her name today. "She was a great cook," said Betty. And "here we are at Mama Galloni's."

FILETTO DI POMODORO

This is Mama Galloni's simple and direct red sauce. She suggests serving it over fresh pasta.

1 (28- or 35-ounce) can imported Italian tomatoes (San Marzano brand preferred)

3 tablespoons olive oil

1 medium onion, chopped

4–6 cloves garlic thinly sliced (about 2 tablespoons)

½ cup red wine

½ teaspoon salt

½ teaspoon pepper

18 fresh basil leaves, torn in large pieces and an additional whole leaf for garnishing each plate

Drain tomatoes (saving the liquid), coarsely chop, and set aside.

Heat the olive oil over medium-high heat. Add the onion and sauté until tender. Add garlic and continue cooking for 1 minute.

Deglaze the pan with the wine, reduce by about half, add tomatoes, the reserved juice, salt and pepper and cook until thickened.

Remove from heat and add fresh basil. Serve over your favorite pasta.

NOTE: Use only fresh basil. Do not substitute with dried.

RECIPE VARIATION

In the height of summer, when fresh vine-ripe tomatoes and basil from your garden are plentiful, peel 8 to 10 medium tomatoes and combine all the ingredients above, eliminating the onion. Let the mixture sit at room temperature for a while (2 to 4 hours is best, but if 15 minutes is all you have, that's okay). This uncooked sauce is great over capellini or angel hair pasta or as a side to whatever may be coming off the grill. Sprinkle with Parmigiano Reggiano or Romano cheese for added pizzazz.

FRESH BASIL PESTO

There has been much debate over making pesto in a mortar and pestle versus the food processor. I have given you both ways. See which one you like better.

No matter which method you use, this pesto keeps nicely in the refrigerator. Simply place it in small containers about 90 percent full and pour a thin layer of olive oil over the top. Cover it and refrigerate or freeze until ready to use.

MAKES ABOUT ½–1 CUP

Pinch of salt

2 cups fresh basil leaves, cleaned and spines removed

2 large garlic cloves, peeled, with the green heart removed

¼ cup toasted pine nuts

2 tablespoons finely grated Parmigiano Reggiano

2 tablespoons finely grated Romano cheese

⅔ cup extra-virgin olive oil, approximately

Salt to taste if necessary

MORTAR AND PESTLE METHOD

Put the salt in the mortar and a few of the basil leaves. Using the pestle (I use a marble mortar and pestle I bought in Italy), crush the leaves and the salt gently but with a firm rhythm against the bottom and sides of the mortar.

Add more leaves a few at a time until they are all used. Add the garlic and crush it with the pestle until it is well mashed. Add the pine nuts and pound them to a paste. Add the cheese, mixing until all ingredients are well combined. Next, add the olive oil a little at a time, stirring with the pestle to form a creamy consistency. You may not need all the oil.

FOOD PROCESSOR METHOD

Use the ingredients from above minus the salt. In a food processor fitted with a steel blade combine the basil and garlic and blend into a fine paste, scrapping down the sides of the bowl when necessary. Add the pine nuts and cheeses, and process until smooth. With the machine running, add the olive oil in a steady stream and mix until smooth and creamy. If sauce is too thick, a little warm water poured through the tube while the machine is running will smooth it out.

LOOKING FOR SOMETHING DIFFERENT?

There are other versions of pesto you could try. For example, use hazelnuts or walnuts instead of pine nuts, or try different herbs such as sage or Italian parsley

JULIA DELLA CROCE'S BROCCOLI RABE PESTO

This recipe from Julia della Croce is a refreshing change from the ubiquitous basil pesto. The cooked broccoli rabe stems contribute body and natural creaminess, making it unnecessary to use as much oil as many pestos call for. As a result, this sauce is lighter, more nutritious, and has a lower calorie count. It's important to peel the broccoli rabe stems before cooking for a silky pesto texture. The almonds add substance and protein, but they are optional. The aged sheep cheese imparts the tanginess we are looking for when using it as a zesty sauce for dried pasta. Besides pasta, use this pesto for coating steamy, freshly boiled potatoes or for topping fish (but leave out the grated cheese).

MAKES ABOUT 1½ CUPS

1 bunch or 1 package pre-washed broccoli rabe

2 tablespoons kosher salt for cooking water, divided

⅓ cup blanched, slivered almonds, lightly toasted (optional)

1 medium clove garlic, minced or shaved

Pinch of hot red pepper flakes or to taste (optional)

¼ cup good extra-virgin olive oil, plus additional for dressing

Fine sea salt to taste

½ cup freshly grated aged and tangy Italian sheep cheese such as Pecorino Romano, or Sardo, plus additional for sprinkling at the table

1 pound imported Italian fusilli

If using bunch broccoli rabe, separate the stems from the crowns. Peel the tough lower stems as you would asparagus and chop the upper portion coarsely; wash in abundant cold water and drain. Use pre-washed greens as is.

Fill an ample pot with enough water to cover the greens and bring it to a rolling boil. Add 1 tablespoon kosher salt, then the broccoli rabe. Cook over high heat until the greens are tender but firm, a total of 1 minute. Use a mesh strainer to lift the greens out of the pot and transfer them to a colander; save the cooking water. Drain the rabe well. Pat dry or whirl in a salad spinner. They should be moist but not wet.

Coarsely grind the almonds if using, garlic, and pepper flakes if using, in a food processor for 10 *to* 15 seconds. Add the drained broccoli rabe and olive oil; pulse to puree until the greens are creamy but still have some texture, about 6 seconds. Taste and add salt if necessary.

Transfer the pesto to a bowl and while it is still warm, fold in the grated cheese.

Bring the broccoli rabe cooking water back to a boil and add the remaining 1 tablespoon kosher salt and the pasta. Follow package directions to cook the pasta *al dente*. Drain and toss with enough of the broccoli rabe pesto to cover lightly, about 6 tablespoons for a pound of fusilli, saving the remaining pesto.

Serve piping hot with an additional thread of olive oil, if desired, and grated cheese at the table.

COOK'S TIP: The ideal pasta for this pesto is fusilli for its ability to trap the creamy sauce between its spirals. Other good matches include orecchiette, penne, linguine, or bucatini. The best quality dried pastas are imported Italian cuts. They're known for their superior wheaty flavor, as well as their ability to retain their elasticity, thus remaining *al dente* (tender but firm to the bite) from pot to table.

"I hated cooking," Mary Ann Esposito said to me. I found these words shocking coming from the host of *Ciao Italia*, the longest-running television cooking program in America,

"I hated cooking from a young age and I'll tell you why," Mary Ann continued, explaining how both of her grandmothers came from the south of Italy—one from Naples, and one from Sicily. Her Neapolitan grandmother was a chef, while her Sicilian grandmother was a butcher. Mary Ann's mother became a dietician. These women were all food professionals, and the extended Italian household revolved around food—good, homemade food. Inside the house, only Italian was spoken. Although I was raised speaking English, this was a milieu I could identify with myself, growing up in an Italian enclave in Sagamore, Massachusetts.

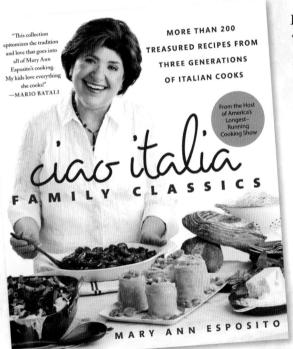

"This collection epitomizes the tradition and love that goes into all of Mary Ann Esposito's cooking. My kids love everything she cooks!"
—MARIO BATALI

MORE THAN 200 TREASURED RECIPES FROM THREE GENERATIONS OF ITALIAN COOKS

From the Host of America's Longest-Running Cooking Show

ciao italia
FAMILY CLASSICS

MARY ANN ESPOSITO

"Everything was made from scratch. Everything," Mary Ann said of her family. "They did not know how to open a can, let me tell you. They squeezed their own tomatoes. We skinned tomatoes 'til the cows came home after my father decided he wanted to plant 100 plants of tomatoes, so there you were."

Like many young people, Mary Ann didn't appreciate until she was an adult just what her family had taught her. "I started to realize what a fabulous heritage I had," she said. "I never appreciated that when I was a teenager. To me it was all drudgery, but now after being in Italy, [I realize that] everything my grandmother had ever told me about Italy was true."

I asked Mary Ann how she felt about the loss of our heritage and where it's going or where it's not going. She said she regrets the loss of the great Italian traditions known to previous generations. "*Ciao Italia* is there to preserve traditional Italian food," she said. "I'm into the real story. This is how our relatives cooked. This is what they cooked. This is how they made it delicious. What's important to me is to keep the traditions alive." She continued by saying, "I don't want to see traditional food die, I see it happening in Italy, as much as I see it happening with our own food culture here."

Mary Ann is sad that most young people no longer cook, either in America or in Italy. "They either get something from the grocery store, or they go out several times a week," she said. "They don't know their own food heritage."

And for Mary Ann, the Italian heritage is bound by food. Take *caponata* for instance, the Sicilian eggplant dish with tomatoes, onions, capers, and olive oil—all ingredients introduced to Sicily. "I usually serve it on semolina bread, which is also classic Sicilian," she said. "To me, we're talking about the history of Sicily."

"Food and culture are central to the Italian-American experience. For generations, Italian-American families have come together around the dinner table where parents and grandparents have passed on their traditions and values. Gaps between generations have been bridged by home-cooked meals."

—MARY ANN ESPOSITO

CAPONATA

Unless you are of Sicilian descent, you might not recognize the word *caponata*. And truth be told there is no firm translation of it other than to say that it is a sweet and sour eggplant relish of sorts. I make a lot of it when my garden is overflowing. *Caponata* can be used for many things. Top some grilled sourdough bread with it or make it the topping to a piece of grilled swordfish or tuna. It is perfect as a sauce for pasta too, and for pizza or focaccia. It's a great vegetarian dish, too, because it is full of good things such as onions, celery, and capers. Another bonus is that *caponata* can be frozen in plastic or glass jars. Come the snows of January, opening a jar of homemade *caponata* can banish those winter blues in a flash.

MAKES ABOUT 9 ½ CUPS

8 (4- or 5-inch) eggplants, washed, trimmed, and cut into 1-inch cubes.

Coarse sea salt

1½ cups water

1¼ cups thinly sliced celery (about 2 ribs)

1½ cups peanut oil, divided

½ cup extra-virgin olive oil

4 onions, thinly sliced (3½ cups)

1 cup tomato paste (use a good brand like Mutti)

1 cup green or black olives in brine, drained and chopped

½ cup capers in wine vinegar, drained

½ cup sugar

⅔ cup red wine vinegar

2 teaspoons baking cocoa

Freshly ground pepper and salt to taste

Place eggplant cubes in a colander, sprinkle with sea salt, and let them sweat in the sink for 1 hour, then rinse and dry them.

In a small saucepan, bring water to a boil. Add celery and cook for 3 or 4 minutes. Drain the celery, saving the water and set aside.

In a large skillet or electric frying pan, heat half the peanut oil. Add as many eggplant pieces as will fit and fry until softened and lightly browned, 12 to 15 minutes. Drain the pieces on brown paper and continue with the remaining eggplant and peanut oil.

In the same skillet, heat the olive oil, add the onions, and sauté until soft and glazed-looking, about 10 minutes. Lower the heat and mix in tomato paste, reserved celery water, olives, capers, sugar, vinegar, and cocoa. Mix well and let the mixture simmer for about 5 minutes.

Add the eggplant and the celery pieces to the skillet and mix well to coat the pieces with the sauce. Simmer the mixture uncovered for about 10 minutes. Add salt and pepper to taste.

Because this recipe makes a lot, I spoon the mixture into jars, cover, and store some in the refrigerator and freeze the rest to be used as needed. You may want to cut this recipe in half, although this *caponata* never lasts long in my house.

COOK'S TIP: Serve the *caponata* in an eggplant that has been cut in half lengthwise and scooped out. Surround the eggplant with slices of semolina bread, lightly fried in a fruity olive oil.

GLOUCESTER MAYOR SEFATIA GIAMBANCO ROMEO THEKEN

Sometimes the memories that a particular dish evokes can be strong enough to bring you to tears and laughter. This is what Sefatia Giambanco Romeo Theken, who was sworn in as the City of Gloucester's Interim Mayor in January 2015, found out.

The dish, a summer favorite in Gloucester, is a mix of linguini, garlic, and fresh Italian ricotta in a cream sauce. It's topped with fried zucchini. The addition of the fried zucchini was Sefatia's idea. It made her mother laugh. "Every time I make it, I cry and think of my mother," Sefatia told me. "I think about her and I can still hear the echo of her laughing. We're laughing and I'm eating and laughing at the same time and people think I'm nuts, but I don't care. Oh my God, here we go, it's summer, kick off the summer."

Gloucester, a fishing town on Cape Ann in Massachusetts, is known as "America's Oldest Seaport." Sefatia is a Gloucester native whose family came from Italy—she still has relatives near Bologna and also in Sicily. She also has the distinction of being the town's first Italian/Sicilian mayor.

Sefatia is affectionately known as "The Godmother of Gloucester." Some say she acquired the nickname because she has 21 godchildren. Others think it is because she was the only woman on the city council. She now prints "Re-Elect The Godmother Sefatia" on her campaign bumper stickers. "Whether I'm a fairy godmother or godmother it doesn't matter, I'm just one of those persons who likes to help people," she says.

Sefatia and I talked about how traditional Italian cooking changed significantly in America. For example, meatballs are not Italian. "It had nothing to do with Italy," Sefatia said. "It had to do with during the war stretching the dollar, trying to fit in. Instead of making a meat sauce they made a meatball."

Throughout the year, Sefatia's family as well as the larger Italian community in the city, celebrate holy days and saint's days Italian-style. The St. Peter's Fiesta is a five-day festival in June honoring St. Peter, the patron saint of fishermen. "[In] July we enjoy the Fourth of July and we do it the Italian way," Sefatia says.

On August 15 the town celebrates *Ferragosto*, a festival with roots in ancient Rome, with picnics held in the Italian community. In Italy, Halloween is All Saints and All Souls Day, and Sefatia follows the Italian tradition of putting shoes behind a door. In December the Italian community commemorates Santa Lucia 12 days before Christmas with Vin Santo cookies. These crunchy *biscotti* soften up when dipped in Vin Santo, a late-harvest dessert wine.

"Every month that there's supposed to be something, we do it," Sefatia said. "It's just an amazing process. The Italian community and the Sicilian community here are just so rich."

GLOUCESTER MAYOR'S FRESH TOMATO, GARLIC, AND BASIL SAUCE

SERVES 4

6 large ripe beefsteak
tomatoes

1 whole head garlic

1 bunch fresh basil, chopped
(about 1½ cups)

½ cup olive oil, or more to
taste

Salt and pepper to taste

1 pound spaghetti, linguini,
or fusilli

Freshly grated Parmigiano
Reggiano cheese

On a wide-toothed grater, grate each of the tomatoes into a
large bowl.

Peel the head of garlic on the outside, getting rid of as much
papery skin as possible, but keeping the head whole. On a
smaller toothed grater, grate the whole head of garlic into
the tomatoes. Add the basil, olive oil, and salt and pepper to
taste, and let sit for at least 10 minutes. (Theken indicated no
amount, but I like the olive oil to show a bit of "sheen," and for
the tomatoes to have a "fat" taste of olive oil.)

Cook the pasta according to the directions, then drain but do
not rinse it. Toss pasta into tomato mixture and toss well.

Serve in bowls. I don't think this pasta needs to be piping hot,
particularly if served in the summer time. The flavors are actually better at room temperature. Pass the cheese if desired.

COOK'S TIP: I reserved ¼ cup of the cooking water and added
it to my sauce. It seemed to work well, but Theken did not
mention it. I think if your tomatoes are very ripe and seasonal,
you will not need to do this, but mine were a bit watery.

SALSA VERDE

This is a wonderful sauce to serve with any boiled or roasted meats or even a simple sautéed fish.

MAKES ABOUT 1 ½ CUPS

¼ cup red wine vinegar

¼ cup water

½ cup chopped stale Italian bread

1 large bunch flat-leaf parsley

2–3 anchovy fillets

1 clove garlic

½ zest from one lemon

¼ cup capers, rinsed and drained

1 hardboiled egg

Several shakes of red pepper flakes

Salt and pepper to taste

Olive oil

In a large bowl, combine vinegar and water. Add bread and allow to soak until soft, 5 to 6 minutes.

On a large cutting board mince the parsley. Add the anchovies, garlic, lemon zest, capers, and egg and continue mincing to a fine texture.

Place chopped mixture into a bowl, add the pepper flakes, salt, pepper, and enough olive oil to combine the mixture.

COOK'S TIP: For best results and a better taste, chop all ingredients by hand instead of using a food processor.

CARBONE'S

88 Franklin Ave.
Hartford, CT 06114
(860) 296-9646
carbonesct.com

Carbone's Ristorante has been an important part of Hartford for over 75 years. Starting as a dream between two brothers in 1936, Carbone's has proved that authentic recipes and a familial atmosphere prosper over all. The restaurant has attracted some large names through the course of history including, Sammy Davis Jr., Dustin Hoffman, and, in more recent years, 50 Cent, Senator Joe Lieberman, and more. When you walk into Carbone's, they make you feel more than welcome, and often treat you better than family.

Carbone's is known to incorporate Old-World hospitality through their tableside preparation. They prepare a few salads and desserts right next to you to show you that each dish is crafted with care. The chefs, including Vinnie Carbone, are truly the backbone of this place, delivering only the freshest ingredients for their homemade meals. They have an extensive and classic Italian menu, coupled with a widespread wine menu and an excellent happy hour selection. Carbone's is a must-go-to historical, delicious, and comfortable spot in the South End of Hartford.

CARBONE'S WINTER CAPRESE SALAD

SERVES 2

4 plum (roma) tomatoes, halved lengthwise

1 shallot, sliced

2 cloves garlic, sliced

2 sprigs of thyme, chopped

1 tablespoon brown sugar

2 teaspoons sherry vinegar

Kosher salt, to taste

Black pepper, to taste

2 tablespoons extra-virgin olive oil, plus more for dressing

2 (4-ounce) fresh mozzarella balls

1 tablespoon basil chiffonade

1 cup baby arugula

Favorite balsamic dressing (optional)

Lemon (optional)

Parmigiano Reggiano cheese (optional)

Divide tomatoes evenly between two bowls. Add shallots, garlic, thyme, brown sugar, and sherry vinegar to each bowl. Season generously with salt and pepper. Pour in olive oil until tomatoes are heavily coated. Mix well.

On sheet pans lined with silicone baking mats or parchment paper, lay out tomatoes evenly, cut side up, in one layer.

Cook at 225°F for 3½ to 4 hours.

Remove tomatoes from oven and let cool to room temperature.

Slice each mozzarella ball into 4 slices each and arrange on plate alternating with tomatoes.

Season mozzarella and tomatoes lightly with salt, pepper, olive oil, and chiffonade basil.

Dress arugula with your favorite balsamic dressing or a simple lemon, olive oil, salt and pepper and top the mozzarella and tomatoes with it, garnish with shaved Parmigiano Reggiano cheese (optional) and serve.

Laura Borghi's pasta machine given to me by her relative.

SECONDI

Pasta, Pizza & Bread

VICTOR COLANGELO

Colangelo Associates Architects
66 Broad Street
Stamford, CT 06901

When Architect Victor Colangelo grew up in Ozone Park, known as the "Little Italy of Queens," the thriving Italian community around him carried on as though the city were a farm.

"People had chickens and goats and stuff like that," he told me. "I remember the chicken coop next door. It was pretty much like a piece of Italy moved here. People had grapevines and made wine. My grandfather made wine here. So we were raised in kind of little Italian town in New York City."

And then there were the city-grown tomatoes. Tomatoes, tomatoes everywhere. In September, as the last of the crop came in, Victor's mother and her friends picked the over-ripe fruit. Then, "they would set up the old drums in the fields, out in the empty lots," Victor said. "They'd set up these steel drums on rocks, on fires, and they'd boil water in these big steel drums. Then they'd pick tomatoes, grind them, put them in old, sterilized bottles, and they had a capping machine and they would cap the bottles." The bottles, wrapped in newspaper, would be lowered into the boiling water to cook. "Everybody would take their share for the winter," he said. "They pickled whatever crops they had. They would either pickle them or somehow preserve them for the winter. That's pretty much the way I was raised."

And did Victor mention the sausage? "They all made sausage through the old traditions. People I know, even in Stamford, still make sausage in their driveway," he said. "The non-Italian wives complain a lot, but they still do it."

Another of Victor's favorite things he remembers his dad making is escarole salad. "Most of our kids don't eat that at all," he said, "but we ate it raw and I still do that pretty much every week." Victor's father, who was raised in Naples, made his salad from the tender inside parts of the escarole head and tossed it with garlic, oil, and vinegar.

"I remember Sundays when I was a little kid," said Victor. "[My dad] would make what people would call today a subway sandwich, or he would mix a salad with cold cuts and an Italian bread. That's what we would have for dinner every Sunday, mixing a salad inside of a sandwich."

Victor's grandmother would make a dandelion salad from dandelions Victor and his grandmother picked in empty lots in Brooklyn and Queens. "We would go look for dandelions and pick a whole bushel," he said. "I haven't made dandelion [salad] in a long time, but I remember that was a real big thing because we could pick it for free."

"It was fantastic to live in that culture," he said. As far as his family's cooking traditions go, Victor still makes pizza, and he even built his own brick oven to do so. "That's something I've always had an enthusiasm for," he said. "My father was a real cook in the family, so I remember a lot of the things he did, I still do." Vincent has many variations for topping his pizzas, " My favorite is the traditional one, San Marzano tomatoes, right from the can, shredded basil, and *bufala mozzarella*." He even offers a bit of advice: "It is important not to put any wet ingredients on the raw pizza dough except for the initial coating of tomatoes and olive oil."

BASIC PIZZA NAPOLETANA DOUGH RECIPE

4 cups all-purpose flour

1½ cups, plus 2–3 tablespoons water

4 teaspoon salt

½ teaspoon dry active yeast

1 teaspoon sugar

Mix all the ingredients together by hand or in a stand mixer slowly for two minutes, until a ball is formed. Let the dough rest for 10 minutes, to allow the flour to absorb the water, then mix at a middle speed (3 or 4 on a mixer) for 5 minutes, and slow for 2 minutes.

Shape the dough into a ball, place it in a slightly oiled bowl, cover it with a towel, and let it rise for 1½ to 2 hours, or until double. Punch it down and push out the air bubbles. Form the dough into a large ball, then cut it into 4 or 5 equal pieces.

Gently shape pieces into a ball, then stretch the top of the ball down and around the rest of the ball until the outer layer wraps around the other side. Pinch the two ends together to make a smooth ball with a tight outer skin. Set your ball seam-side down, dust with flour, and store them under a damp towel, in a proofing tray, or under plastic wrap. This will prevent the outside of the ball from drying out and creating a crust, thus making it difficult to work. The top of the pizza ball should be soft and silky.

Your balls of dough will need to rest for about an hour to become soft and elastic, which makes them easily stretched into a thin crust pizza.

If you don't need your balls of dough for a few hours, you should refrigerate them, and bring them back out of the refrigerator an hour or so before you want to use them.

MAMMA GALLONI'S PASTA DOUGH

2 cups all-purpose flour

3 extra-large eggs (room temperature) slightly beaten

1 teaspoon extra-virgin olive oil

Pinch of salt

Pour flour into a medium-size bowl or onto a work surface. Make a well in the center of the flour and add the eggs, oil, and salt. Mix with a fork. Mixture should form a stiff dough. Add a drop of water if necessary. Knead the dough for 10 to 15 minutes, until it is smooth and firm, and quite elastic. Place the dough on a lightly floured plate and cover it with an inverted bowl. Let it rest for 1 hour at room temperature.

With a pasta machine or by hand roll dough out to desired thinness.

THE FIRST PIZZA IN SOUTHERN NEW HAMPSHIRE

As hard as it is to believe today, there was a time not so long ago when people in the small New Hampshire town of Amherst had never heard of pizza.

Marlene Cocchi Baldwin told me the story of how Adamo's Restaurant introduced pizza to Amherst in the mid-1950s. The family-run restaurant was owned and operated by Baldwin's aunt Olga Cocchi Adamo and her husband Bruno Adamo for more than 40 years.

Olga and Bruno were both born in and lived in Plymouth, Massachusetts. When Bruno's parents, Battista and Josephine, were laid off at the Cordage Company in Plymouth, they moved to New Hampshire and opened an ice cream shop in Amherst. Battista made the ice cream and Josephine ran the shop. As the shop's popularity grew, people asked if there was anything else to eat. To feed them, Josephine decided to prepare spaghetti with her homemade red sauce, which she cooked on her apartment stove. Things were a success until, sadly, in 1956, a truck spun out-of-control on an icy New Hampshire road and killed Battista.

To help his mother in the shop, Bruno, married to Olga by now, left his job as a presser at Puritan Clothing Company in Plymouth. The couple, along with Peter, their three-year-old son, moved to Amherst.

Josephine then had a brainstorm: Why not sell pizza? The townspeople had never heard of pizza. Word spread about the new pizzeria in town, and the pizza immediately became a big success. In fact, it was so successful that Olga and Bruno bought the building across the street to mass-produce frozen pizzas—something unheard of at the time. The small ice cream parlor was now a full-service restaurant with an Italian menu and full liquor license. Bruno made the pizzas in the bakery and was known as "Bruno the King of Pizza." Olga made the entrees and desserts and sometimes acted as the bartender. When he was old enough, Peter worked alongside his father baking pizzas. Josephine, too, continued working until she retired. In the late 1990s Bruno and Olga sold the business and retired to Florida. Olga passed away at the age 87 in 2012. Bruno, her husband of 66 years, still lives in Florida.

DIMILLO'S ON THE WATER

25 Long Wharf
Portland, ME 04101
(207) 772-2216
dimillos.com/restaurant

DiMillo's is a multi-generation family restaurant in Portland, Maine. "I have been working in the family business since I was eight," Steve DiMillo told me on a frigid winter day. "My first job was washing dishes, and I worked in every aspect of this business."

Steve's father Tony first ran a store and then, in 1954, opened a restaurant called Anthony's. Tony coined the slogan "The clams you eat here today slept last night in Casco Bay." DiMillo's, which was established in 1965, still uses that slogan to this day to describe its sparkling fresh seafood.

In 1999, when Tony died at the age of 66, Steve and other family members took over managing the business. "This restaurant was my father's dream," Steve said. In his office we talked about his father's life and career in the restaurant world of Portland.

The boat, which houses the restaurant, began its life as a car ferry in 1941 and has had many incarnations since. Tony purchased it in 1980 and opened it as a restaurant in 1982 when it was the only floating restaurant on the Upper East Coast. The boat is situated right in the middle of Portland Harbor and offers spectacular water views. His father's original idea was to have a restaurant at the end of the pier, but he later came up with the concept of a restaurant directly in the harbor.

While Steve and I were talking, Steve's mother Arlene arrived. The three of us talked about the family's Italian history and the restaurant her husband Tony started. Arlene still works in the restaurant alongside Steve. Tony's 85-year-old sister Justina also works at the restaurant's front desk during the evening.

Both of Tony's and Justina's parents were born in different parts of Abruzzo, Italy. "I was born and raised here in Portland," Justina said. "My father Eugene immigrated to Canada from Italy, then came and settled in Lewiston, Maine, where his brother lived." Eugene then moved to the "big city" of Portland and found the Italian neighborhood where many people from the Abruzzo area had settled near St. Peters Church.

Their mother Rose came here with her parents when she was 16, and met her future husband, Eugene. "There were two boys, Tony, John, and [us] four girls: Mary, Adele, Jeanette, and myself in our family. Everyone in our family spoke Italian because our grandparents and parents all spoke Italian. We didn't speak English until we went to school," she recalled.

When asked about what foods she remembers and likes the best, she answered, "Well, do you know polenta? We call it *la polenta*. It is served on a large board topped with a red sauce and freshly grated cheese then placed in the middle of the table and everyone digs in! Sometimes we add our favorite homemade meatballs or sausage."

Justina remembers her grandfather selling sausage made by her grandmother and mother in the grocery store they owned. She says that people all over Portland came to buy them.

"You can't find that anymore, nobody makes them like they did," Justina said. She also remembers helping out with the process. "We used to go to the store and they would grind the pork—pure pork, beautiful—add the spices, and keep mixing by hand! Then us—the children—had to put the pork in the machine until it came out in the casing. It was fun and I have fond memories of this."

BASIC LA POLENTA

MAKES ENOUGH TO SERVE
6-8 PEOPLE

1¾ cup yellow cornmeal

2 cups cold water

1 teaspoon salt

3 tablespoons olive oil

Combine cornmeal, water, and salt in a bowl and set aside.

In a large pot, bring 5 cups of water to a boil. Add the oil and stir in the cornmeal. With an electric or hand beater, beat the cornmeal until it starts to thicken (3 to 4 minutes). This will keep the *polenta* smooth and free of lumps. Cook it over medium heat, stirring constantly with a wooden spoon for 20 to 30 minutes.

Turn off heat, cover the pot and shake it a little. This will allow some steam to get under the *polenta* so it will detach itself from the bottom of the pot, making clean up easier. Let the *polenta* stay on the stove for 3 to 5 minutes without stirring it.

Depending on how you are going to use it, you can either pour the *polenta* out onto a board, or pour it in a large bowl, let it cool, and slice it with a knife. It is also good served the next morning, sliced and dipped in a little olive oil and butter, topped with Parmigiano Reggiano cheese and a fried egg.

WOLF MEADOW FARM

91 High St.
Amesbury, MA 01913
(978) 201-1606
wolfmeadowfarm.com

Wolf Meadow Farm cheesemaker Luca Mignogna sometimes drives out to the barn to get fresh, unpasteurized milk straight from a cow at 3 a.m. While there, he visits with the cows, whom he calls his "ladies."

"Those are beautiful creatures. They do better if you actually work with them," Luca said. He claims he is building a relationship with the cows. "I know that they know that I do something with the milk. I don't think they have a clear idea with cheesemaking, but they know that I'm using the milk. I say, 'Thank you, ladies,' every time I get the milk. 'I love you.' They look at you."

Wolf Meadow Farm obtains all of its milk from the Artichoke Dairy in West Newbury, Massachusetts. From this, according to the season, Luca creates traditional southern Italian farm cheeses such as ricotta, caciocavallo, scamorza, and many others. Luca also offers cheesemaking classes.

Luca grew up on a farm in Campobasso, the capital of Molise, Italy, in the middle of the Apennines. There he learned to make cheese in an age-old, sustainable fashion. In 2003 Luca moved to California and became involved with running two restaurants. As he grew more interested in organic foods, he bought some raw milk and made farmer's cheese, and then mozzarella. His artisan cheeses became popular in the restaurant. "I was spending more time doing cheese than actually being at the restaurant," he said.

In 2008, when his father died, the 18-hour trip to Italy seemed too long. So Luca moved to the Boston area and began hunting for a place to make his cheeses. After a long search, he ended up in the small town of Amesbury. "We were really happy when we found this location," he said.

About his cheesemaking, Luca says, "I'm not a magician, I cannot use bad product and make something unique. These products are unique because of the good quality of the milk, and this is crucial." Luca insists that the way for cows to produce high-quality milk is to enjoy "a serene life in a barn, where the ladies are really treated well." He says if you provide "just quiet, a little bit of music, pet the animals," he said.

"They know if you are upset, they know if you're serene. They know if you're going to pet them, they know if you're going to be aggressive. They feel it."

When I asked him if he learned these attitudes in Italy when he was growing

up on the family farm, he explained, "When you're coming from a generation of farmers, you grow with the habit of treating the animals well, because your father does, because your grandfather does, because your great-grandfather does," he said. "We grew with those animals, and we understood that they were part of the family because they were feeding the family—with eggs, with meat, with everything."

While Luca has enjoyed success here in America with his artisan cheeses, the irony is that in Italy, Luca told me, the old cheesemaking traditions are dying because they are too labor-intensive. "It's not worth it because they [have] to pay too much and there are so many people there," he said. For example, a machine can be used to stretch the Caciocavallo cheese, but Luca believes in the old method, *fatto a mano*, or made by hand. Although he owns two of the machines to stretch and ball cheese, he doesn't use them, partly because "they don't have the ability to love."

BUCATINI WITH CHEESE AND PEPPER

Cacio e Pepe con Bucatini (Bucatini with Cheese and Pepper) is one of Rome's simplest pasta dishes that has become trendy. When made right, this dish is incredible. The authentic recipe calls for only three ingredients: Pecorino Romano cheese, black pepper, and pasta. This is Luca's version of this dish made with his own ricotta cheese.

SERVES 4-6

1–3 tablespoons extra-virgin olive oil

½ yellow onion diced

¼ cup dry white wine

1 pound bucatini pasta

1 teaspoon salt

½ pound Wolf Meadow Farm Ricotta (or other good quality ricotta)

Cracked fresh pepper to taste

¼ pound grated Pecorino cheese

Heat olive oil in a sauté pan, add the onion, and cook until slightly brown. Add the white wine and cook until it evaporates.

Place the pasta in a large pot of boiling water with a teaspoon of salt. Cook until *al dente*. Drain pasta, reserving ½ to 1 cup of the cooking water.

Add the water to the onions along with the ricotta cheese and black pepper and stir until well combined.

Add the cooked pasta and more black pepper if desired.

Serve immediately in warm bowls, topped with Pecorino Romano cheese.

CONSIGLIO'S

165 Wooster St.
New Haven, CT 06511
(203) 865-4489
consiglios.com

Annunziata and Salvatore Consiglio opened this small neighborhood Italian restaurant on New Haven's famed Italian-centric Wooster Street more than 75 years ago, and their grandchildren and great grandchildren continue their legacy.

After immigrating to the Wooster Street area from Amalfi, Italy, Annunziata and Salvatore opened their first restaurant, "The Big Apple," steps away from their home, and enlisted the help of their eight children to operate the restaurant. The family worked long hours as chefs, hosts, bartenders, waiters, kitchen help, and everything in between, and the restaurant's good reputation and popularity grew, extending

beyond the neighborhood and becoming a New Haven favorite. When New Haven's redevelopment program forced the restaurant to move, the family changed the name to "Consiglio's" and moved a few doors down to its current address.

CONSIGLIO'S CAVATELLI PASTA

MAKES 7 POUNDS

8 cups flour, extra for dusting

3 pounds ricotta cheese

6 eggs

1 tablespoon salt

2 ounces vegetable oil

Add all ingredients to a large mixing bowl and blend until combined and dough begins to form. Knead by hand for a few minutes until all ingredients are fully combined and can form a workable ball.

Break dough into smaller sections (about the size of a tennis ball) and roll by hand into "snakes." You can add extra flour if dough becomes too sticky to work with.

Cut snakes into 1-inch sections. If desired, use a pastry cutter or fork to imprint a design on the pasta.

Boil in salted water for 5 to 7 minutes until pasta floats to the top. Drain and toss with your favorite sauce. Don't worry if you have lots of pasta left over, this recipe freezes well! (To freeze, divide the pasta into portion size bundles. Place on a cookie sheet lined with parchment or waxed paper. Partially air dry the pasta bundles, then place in the freezer for a few hours or until they have hardened. Remove and place in freezer bags then place back in the freezer. The pasta will keep for several months.)

GNOCCHI WITH BROWN BUTTER

This brown butter sauce may also be used over vegetables such as string beans, cauliflower, and butternut squash.

SERVES 2 AS A DINNER
OR 4 AS A SIDE DISH

½ teaspoon salt

1 package potato gnocchi, fresh or frozen

8–9 tablespoons unsalted butter cut into small pieces

16–17 fresh sage leaves

1 teaspoon lemon zest

Salt and pepper to taste

Bring a large pot of well-salted water to a boil over high heat. Add the gnocchi batches several at a time and stir gently. When they float to the top, remove with a slotted spoon to a colander. Repeat process until all are used. Cover to keep warm.

Place a large skillet over high heat and add the butter. When the butter has almost completely melted, stir in the sage leaves, Cook, stirring until the butter turns a light brown color (do not let the butter burn) and the sage leaves darken slightly about 2 to 3 minutes.

Add the reserved gnocchi to the pan with the lemon zest and toss to coat well and heat until the gnocchi are warm. Season with salt and freshly ground pepper to taste.

Serve immediately in warm bowls

BALBONI'S BAKERY

25 King St., Agawam MA 01001, (413) 786-4514

In my village in Sagamore where I grew up, Louis Market was the hub for news, gossip, and Italian foods. In the cellar of the market was a bakery where owner Louis Conconi would make bread from a recipe originating in Northern Italy. It was referred to as "Horn" or "Star" bread. This finely textured bread baked in the shape of four horns was a staple on the Italian table at each meal. It was never thrown away, but always used in one way or another. Odd stale pieces were soaked in water, cooked in a little olive oil with a little salt and pepper, served in a bowl with freshly grated Parmigiano Reggiano cheese, and eaten as a meal called *pun cott* (from the Italian *pane cotto,* which means cooked bread), or it was crushed into bread crumbs. My grandfather even dunked it in his coffee in the morning.

This "horn" bread played an important role in my childhood. I remember when I was six running to the bakery on Saturday mornings for the fresh dough that my mother fashioned into sweet fried "doughboys," made with her special cookie cutter in the shape of a boy, and dusted with cinnamon sugar. This was a special treat! Sometimes the dough was turned into a pizza, topped with my mother's simple red sauce that cooked on the stove for several hours.

Many years later, the bakery closed and John Bulla, who had married Louis's daughter Jenny, bought the store. The only source they had for the bread was the Balboni

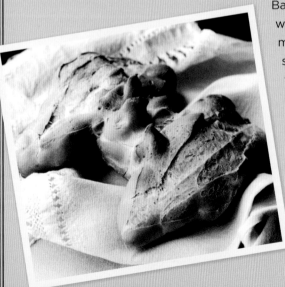

Bakery in Plymouth, Massachusetts. Jenny would travel to Plymouth every Saturday morning to obtain the bread to sell in the store. This went on for several years until the Balboni Bakery closed, and the secret recipe was lost.

By some coincidence, when I took a trip to Massachusetts, I found a bakery called Balboni's in Agawan, which had no relation or connection to the Balboni's in Plymouth. Located in a residential area, the bakery was marked by a little sign that pointed to a small building in the back of a driveway. There it was, a familiar, very Old World, four-generation family tradition being kept alive with love and caring for what they believed in.

The bakery is owned and run by May and Ken Balboni along with their children. May was a former schoolteacher and Ken started working in the bakery as a child with his father, who started it in 1912.

As I opened the door and entered the store, I was greeted by the smell of freshly baked bread and the sight of shelves lined with the familiar "horn" bread, large and small, and bags of assorted homemade pasta.

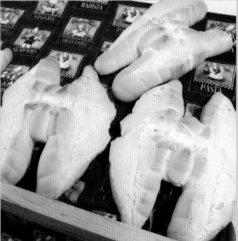

May was at the counter happily greeting a customer. When she was finished, I introduced myself and we talked briefly. Then she escorted me back to the bakery to meet Ken, who was baking bread sticks in the oversized rotating oven. In my conversation with May, I asked if I could have the recipe for the bread.

"Oh no, this is a secret recipe! We would never give it out!" she said. May and Ken take pride in carrying on the Old World tradition of bread making, which has not changed for 100 years.

LINGUINE WITH BROCCOLI RABE AND SHRIMP

Seafood is not an ingredient usually associated with broccoli rabe, the bitter greens so loved by southern Italians, but here is a dish I love to make. It combines them with linguine and shrimp and was given to me by Julia della Croce, print and broadcast journalist and National Public Radio contributor. Julia is also the recipient of the 2015 M.F.K. Fisher Award for Excellence as well as a cookbook author and culinary consultant to many.

SERVES 4 AS A FIRST COURSE

1 bunch broccoli rabe or equivalent weight of pre-washed bagged broccoli rabe

2 tablespoon kosher salt

7 tablespoons extra-virgin olive oil

6 large garlic cloves, smashed

¼ teaspoon hot red pepper flakes

½ pound medium or large shrimp, shelled, deveined, and patted dry with paper towels

¼ teaspoons fine sea salt

¼ cup dry white wine

½ pound good quality imported Italian linguine

SPECIAL EQUIPMENT: large mesh strainer or kitchen "spider"

If using bunch broccoli rabe, trim off any discolored tips from the bottom of the stems. Sever the stems from the tops and cut them into 2-inch lengths while leaving the buds whole. Wash the greens in abundant cold water. Use pre-washed bag broccoli rabe as is.

In large stockpot, bring 6 quarts water and the salt to a rolling boil. Add broccoli rabe and cook for 2½ minutes. Place a large mixing bowl next to the burner, using the strainer lift the greens out all at once and set the strainer over the bowl to drain. Set aside. Reserve the cooking water.

In the meantime, in a skillet large enough to accommodate the cooked greens and the pasta later, warm 3 tablespoons of the olive oil over medium-low heat. Stir in half the garlic and red pepper flakes and sauté gently until the garlic is colored but not brown, about 3 minutes. Add the drained greens to the skillet and push them around in the oil to coat evenly. Transfer them to a warm bowl and use a paper towel to wipe the skillet clean.

Warm the remaining oil with the remaining garlic over medium-low heat until it is golden but not brown. Add the shrimp to the pan and sauté until pink on both sides, about 6 minutes. Take care not to overcook them. Add the sea salt and wine, and toss shrimp in the liquid to enable them to absorb it evenly. Turn the heat to low and simmer for another minute to allow the alcohol to evaporate.

Add the greens to the skillet and toss them together with the shrimp. Fish the garlic out or leave it in, as you prefer. Set the skillet aside.

Bring the reserved broccoli rabe cooking water back to a rapid boil. Stir in the linguine and cook precisely according to the package instructions for *al dente*. Drain and toss the pasta together with the broccoli rabe and shrimp. Taste to adjust salt and serve piping hot.

FRANK PEPE'S PIZZERIA NAPOLETANA

157 Wooster St.
New Haven, CT 06511
(203) 865-5762
pepespizzeria.com

Like most kids whose families run a restaurant, Francis Rosselli, a co-owner of Frank Pepe's Pizzeria, began as a young teen working in the business his grandfather Frank Pepe founded in 1925.

Today Frank Pepe's is one of the best-known pizzerias in the country. In fact, in 2013 Frank Pepe's was named the *best* pizza in the entire nation, and its white clam pie and other pizzas consistently make the Best 101 national pizza lists. Words like "legendary" are used to describe Frank Pepe's mouth-watering pizza. Yet the business grew from humble beginnings on Wooster Street in New Haven.

Francis told me a bit about the family's origins when we met in the second location of Frank Pepe's at 157 Wooster Street. The family opened an annex pizzeria in

Frank Pepe's original location at 163 Wooster Street in the late 1970s. That location, known as The Spot, is open only on Friday evenings and weekends.

Frank Pepe hailed from Maiori, on Italy's Amalfi Coast. When he arrived in New Haven in 1909, joining his brother Allecio, he was poor and illiterate, and went to work in a factory. He returned to Italy to fight for his homeland in World War I. While there after the war, he married Filomena Volpi, a girl from his hometown, and together they returned to New Haven in 1920.

After working for a macaroni manufacturer, Frank opened a bakery and hawked his bread in the streets from a cart. Eventually he sold the bread only from his bakery. In 1925 it was a natural progression for Frank and Filomena to bake and sell a traditional food of Naples—pizza pies.

"Originally he started with the two simple pies, two simple pieces," Francis said. "One with what we call the original tomato pie right now, which was simply crushed tomatoes with Pecorino Romano grated cheese, oil, garlic, and oregano. The other was with anchovies. It came before mozzarella and all the rest of the ingredients that are so common to us now. That's how he started." Frank is credited with originating what is known as the New Haven–style thin crust.

The area around Wooster Street boasted a large Italian community, and Frank fit right in. "My grandfather was a very likeable man," Francis recalled. "Very, very likable. As he became successful, he was quite the guy around town. A very unassuming guy, but very, very well liked. Loved, actually."

Through the years, the family-owned business expanded, with other close relatives joining in. Frank and Filomena lived on the third floor of the building above the pizzeria with their two daughters, Elizabeth and Serafina. The girls worked in the

business just as the seven children of Elizabeth and Serafina do today. The business has expanded to six locations in Connecticut and one in New York.

Francis, who was born in 1952, has fond memories of weekly family dinners hosted by his grandmother Filomena, whom he describes as a "fabulous cook." On Thanksgiving Frank would roast a turkey and serve it with a soft "moscia" bread that was baked from pizza dough.

"It's a very moist dough that we use, so that bread also was a very moist bread, not a dry Italian loaf as you customarily would think," Francis said. "It's a lovely bread for a change, you know?"

As well as the original tomato pie and the white clam pie, Pepe's offers a pizza margherita with crushed Italian tomatoes and fresh mozzarella and basil. Another specialty pizza is a fresh spinach, mushroom, and gorgonzola pie. Toppings include pepperoni, onions, and peppers as well as the more daring shrimp and oven-roasted chicken. Frank Pepe's has become so well known, in fact, that it also sells souvenir mugs and clothing sporting the name of Frank Pepe.

GELATO GIULIANA

110 Food Terminal Plaza, New Haven, CT 06511
(203) 772-0607, gelatogiuliana.com

Giuliana Maravelle opened her own Italian cafe and was interested in finding an authentic gelato to serve. After trying dozens of options, she knew none of them reflected the true crafted artisan gelato she ate as a child in Italy. Determined to have her café sell this kind of gelato, she bought her own small machine and made it herself. The response was overwhelming. People came in on a daily basis asking for hand-packed pints to take home. Giuliana and her staff couldn't keep up with the demand! She rented a small warehouse to produce her heavenly gelato and eventually began distributing locally. Now, nine years later, Gelato Giuliana has spread out, now supplying her product to most of the east coast. This is a family-operated business, and many of its employees have been involved since the business started.

What keeps the people coming back? What makes *this* gelato so special? Giuliana says they have never compromised any of the ingredients they use, despite the fact that doing so could greatly lower their costs. They seek only the best for their gelato and customers, getting many of their ingredients right from Italy—their cocoa powder comes from Perugia, their pistachios from Sicily, and they use only the best American-grown fruits. The passion that goes into making this gelato is undoubtedly what separates it from the rest.

VENDA RAVIOLI

265 Atwells Ave., Providence, RI 02903, (401) 421-9105
vendaravioli.com

Venda Ravioli, in the middle of Atwells Avenue on Federal Hill in Providence, Rhode Island, is a landmark in the area. The store is located on the corner of the beautiful DePasquale Plaza, which boasts a fountain, specialty shops, and a small hotel. Mary and David Venteroni established Venda in 1938. The 200-square-foot food shop grew into a large emporium after Alan Costantino purchased Venda Ravioli in 1972. Today it is a bustling Italian gourmet store.

In the morning, customers congregate for their morning coffee and pastry at the espresso bar. Then there's the large glassed-in counter that runs the length of the store featuring a huge assortment of Italian prepared foods—everything from salads to flavorful cooked meats and chicken dishes, chicken Parmesan or cutlets, fried eggplant plain or eggplant Parmesan, lasagna, and many more entrees and appetizers to choose from. Any of these items can be eaten there or be taken out. As you make your way around the large center counter toward the meat section, there are butchers making sausages, hot or mild. Next you find an assortment of olives, marinated vegetables, and your choice of imported and domestic cheeses; it is quite amazing. This is the place to sample some of their selection. If you have a desire for a pasta dish, lining the wall to the left of the store, is a vast selection of frozen fresh pastas, gnocchi, raviolis, manicotti, and tortellini. The aisles of the store are also filled with imported Italian products.

During warmer weather Venda offers outdoor dining on the square in front of the fountain, complete with live Italian music. Chef Salvatore Cefaliello and his staff preside in the kitchen.

On the opposite corner, across from Venda Ravioli, is the Venda Bar & Restaurant (401-528-1100), which is open for dinner seven days a week. It serves the dinner version of the food offered across the way at Venda Ravioli. The restaurant is on two floors and has an extensive Italian wine list and as well as offerings of others from around the world. Chef Chiero is the chef in the kitchen and creates delicious pizza baked in an authentic oven imported from Italy.

VENDA'S
ANTIPASTO SALAD
$6·99

MARINATED
ARTICHOKE
HEARTS

IMPORTED
ONIONS
(GRILLED)
$14.99 LB

100 Disposable Gloves

MEZZA LUNA

253 Main St.
Buzzards Bay, MA 02532
(508) 759-4667
mezzalunarestaurant.com

"In this business, you have to evolve with the times," says Emilio John (E.J.) Cubellis II, third-generation owner of Mezza Luna. E.J.'s grandmother, Speranza Cubellis, and his father, Johnny Cubellis, opened this family-run Italian restaurant in Buzzard's Bay in 1937. "Now with the local people, they're so used to my menu that when they hear something different, they try it and they trust me because I don't put anything on a plate that I don't like myself, or don't agree with."

E.J. began working at the restaurant as a teenager. "I did dishes, prep work, whatever it was," he says. "Basically we lived next door and I would be over here with my father."

E.J. attended Johnson & Wales University to study restaurant management in the 1990s. His father was already in his mid-70s by then, and the restaurant had fallen into hard times due to a tough economy. The completion of Route 25, which diverted traffic bound for Cape Cod around Buzzard's Bay, didn't help either. So when E.J. joined his father at the restaurant, he worked six or seven days a week for two or three years with scarcely a day off. And if you think things went smoothly with his father, think again.

"We had our arguments, plenty of them, father and son," E.J. said. "I had some ideas that I wanted to bring to the table and he was a stubborn old Italian guy that didn't agree with it. I give you a perfect example: mussels."

E.J.'s dad came from Naples, and most everything in Naples is prepared in tomato sauce, including the mussels. "I had a recipe for some mussels and it was in a cream

sauce with some garlic and
he argued with me for three
days," E.J. said. "'That's not
how you serve them; that's
not how they're supposed
to be prepared.' he said.
I told him, 'I think the
people like them.'"

After Johnny finally agreed
to allow E.J. to serve the mussels any way he liked, E.J. offered a
mussel special serving the mussels in the creamy garlic sauce. "I probably sold a hundred orders over the course of a week and a half," he recalled. In contrast, he sold six
orders of the mussels in marinara sauce. When he and his father conferred about the
mussels, and his father realized that the mussels in cream sauce were outselling the
ones in tomato sauce, he agreed that E.J. could list mussels any way he wanted on the
menu. "I think that was a good turning point for him to realize that being stubborn
wasn't going to help, and change is okay," E.J. said.

So, while Mezza Luna always keeps staple dishes such as stuffed shells, veal,
chicken, and eggplant Parmesan on the menu, "We bring new things to the table
now," E.J. said. "We do a stuffed pork chop that people go crazy for. We just recently
offered asparagus wrapped in fresh prosciutto with fresh mozzarella, pan-fried, and
we put a little balsamic glaze over it." They made 82 orders of the dish before selling
out. "The wait staff loves to sell them because it's different, it's new," E.J. added.

E.J. bought the business from his father when he was about 25, and his father 80.
"The rewards you get in this business—they're not monetary. But, you do get a nice
reward when you roam the dining room at the end of the night and you see your
customers and they thank you," he said. "They thank you because they enjoyed their
meal. They enjoyed the service; they enjoyed the atmosphere."

SHELLS STUFFED WITH SPINACH

MAKES ABOUT 35 STUFFED SHELLS
AND SERVES 8-10

1 pound spinach

2 cups ricotta cheese

4 ounces cream cheese

¼ teaspoon grated nutmeg, or
more to taste

Salt and pepper

1 egg, lightly beaten

1 (12-ounce) package) jumbo
pasta shells (approximately
35–36 per package)

Fifteen-Minute Fresh Tomato
Sauce (see page 46)

Remove any tough center ribs from spinach. Wash, but do not dry. With only the water left clinging to the leaves, cook in a large pot for a few minutes to wilt the leaves. Drain and squeeze completely dry. Finely chop the spinach.

In a medium bowl beat together spinach, ricotta, cream cheese, and nutmeg until smooth. Salt and pepper to taste. Then beat in the egg.

Prepare the shells according to package; drain and rinse with cold water to cool and carefully set aside. Lightly butter a shallow baking dish large enough to hold the shells in one layer. Stuff shells with about 1 tablespoon of cheese mixture each.

Arrange in baking dish. Cover with sauce. Bake at 350°F for about 25 minutes until heated through.

SHELLS STUFFED WITH WINTER SQUASH

I love to recreate many of the recipes I remember from growing up in an Italian-American village. Sometimes I do my own version. This one is filled with a medley of winter squashes and another with a combination of Swiss chard leaves and ricotta cheese. I learned this from my surrogate mother, Rose Sorenti. These are delicious topped with my Fifteen-Minute Fresh Tomato Sauce (see page 46).

MAKES ABOUT 35 SHELLS
AND SERVES 10

2½ cups (about 3 pounds) cooked winter squash such as butternut, hubbard, acorn, buttercup, or pumpkin (any or all of the combinations work well.)

½ cup water

2 tablespoons butter

¼ teaspoon nutmeg

½ cup Parmigiano Reggiano cheese

Dash white pepper

Salt

1 (12-ounce) package) jumbo pasta shells (approximately 35–36 per package)

Tomato sauce

Preheat oven to 375°F.

Wash the squash, cut into quarters, and place in a baking dish skin side up. Add water and bake for 1 hour or until soft.

Remove from oven, let cool slightly, scoop out the pulp and place in a food processor fitted with a steel blade (it is important that the squash be fairly dry). Add butter, nutmeg, and cheese, and process until pureed. Adjust seasonings; add salt only if necessary.

Prepare shells according to package directions; drain carefully and set aside to cool slightly. Lightly butter a shallow baking dish large enough to hold the shells in one layer.

Stuff each shell with about 1½ tablespoons of squash mixture. Arrange in baking dish. Cover with your choice of tomato sauce and bake for 20 minutes until heated through.

PENNE PASTA ALLA CARBONARA

MAKES 4 SERVINGS

1 pound penne pasta

¼ cup diced pancetta

1 medium onion, chopped

1 stick butter

1 pint heavy cream, warmed

1 cup peas

Salt, pepper, and red pepper flakes, to taste

In a pot of salted boiling water, cook the pasta until *al dente*. Drain and set aside to cool.

In a large saucepan, sauté the pancetta until the fat is rendered. Add the onions and cook until translucent. Lower the heat and add the butter. When melted, add the heavy cream and reduce until thick. Add the peas and cooked pasta. Season with salt, pepper, and red pepper flakes. Serve hot with a slice of ciabatta bread.

PLYMOUTH CORDAGE COMPANY

In 1824 The Plymouth Cordage Company was founded. It was a rope making company located in Plymouth, Massachusetts. By the 19th century, it had become the largest manufacture of rope in the world. It was also a place where Italian immigrants come to work. Many came from Cento and Renazzo Italy where they had worked in the factories there. The Plymouth Cordage Company played a small role in the Sacco and Vanzetti case (see "Boston's Little Italy" on page 18) because Bartolomeo Vanzetti worked there in the early part of the 1900's.

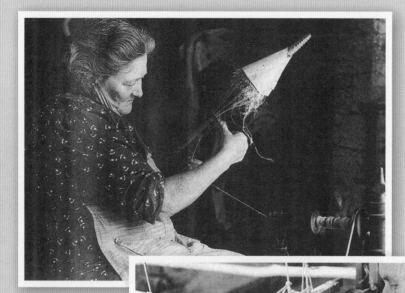

Women working in the rope factory in Cento Italy.

BRUNO TROPIANO

When Bruno Tropiano Sr. retired, he found he had more time to return to his Italian roots. Bruno was born in Avellino in Campania, south of Naples. In 1969, after he finished a stint in the Italian army, he immigrated to the Bronx in New York where he joined his father Benjamin, his mother Philomena, and his three younger brothers.

While going to school at night, he worked in a machine shop. Later, when he moved to Danbury, Connecticut, he worked his way up at Jovil Manufacturing, eventually buying the company in 1983. In 2014, he sold the company and retired.

"I've got my house. I've got my garden. I've got my chickens," he said. "I've spent time with my chickens. I get fresh eggs every day. Then I do my garden." Bruno returns to Italy every year for six weeks, where he and his nonagenarian father make wine together.

In 2001, Bruno began his deep involvement with the Amerigo Vespucci Lodge, which was established under the Order of the Sons of Italy in 1924. He is the group's current president and, as such, helps the entire town of Danbury honor its Italian roots.

"We have about three hundred members. It's a good club," he said. "We do the Italian Festival. We do Columbus Day. We do a Christmas party, a children's Christmas party."

The lodge's Tuesday night pasta dinner is open to the community for $8. The group also runs picnics for seniors. Bruno even organized a fundraiser for people in Italy affected by an earthquake.

"It's like an American dream," he said about the arc of his life—arriving in America and eventually owning his own business and prospering enough to put his three children through college. Yet through it all, the family remembers its Italian roots—Bruno's son Bruno Jr. went to a top business college, Bentley University, and is a co-founder of Gelato Fiasco in Maine (see page 188).

SPAGHETTI WITH WHITE CLAM SAUCE

This is a basic recipe for Bruno Tropiano's pasta with clams. You can embellish this dish by adding crispy sliced garlic chips, or, if you would like a red sauce, mix a tablespoon or two into the wine and clam juice.

SERVES 2

½ pound spaghetti

¼ cup olive oil

1 tablespoon butter

3–4 cloves garlic, minced

1 small hot red pepper, sliced or red pepper flakes to taste

¼ cup dry white wine

½ cup clam juice

¾ cup minced clams

6 small clams, 3 per person

¾ cup finely chopped fresh Italian parsley

Zest of ½ lemon

Bring a large pot of salted water to a boil and cook pasta until *al dente.*

Meanwhile, heat the olive oil and butter in a saucepan over medium-high heat. Add the garlic and pepper and cook for 2 to 3 minutes until softened.

Add the wine and clam juice and bring to a boil, 2 to 3 minutes.

Stir in minced clams, small clams, parsley, and lemon zest. Drain the pasta and add to the saucepan. Serve immediately in warm bowls.

CHEF'S TIP: Steam the clams in ½ cup white wine and use the stock in the base. This will insure their freshness and you will not destroy the dish if one clam is filled with sand. Discard any that do not open. The clams should be added last to just heat them through.

SIMONE'S

275 Child St.
Warren RI 02885
(401) 247-1200
SimonesRI.com

I met Chef Joe Simone at his stylish new restaurant just outside of Providence, on the same cold rainy day I was heading home from exploring Federal Hill's Little Italy. It was mid-afternoon and his outgoing, friendly staff was sharing a family-style meal together before preparing food for the evening dinner menu. I sat down with him and we started talking about his background and how he became interested in food.

"I grew up in a family where everyone cooked in the Italian tradition way. My Italian father did most of the cooking because he liked to cook and my mother didn't much enjoy it," he said.

Simone moved from New Jersey to Rhode Island with his family in 1976. At the time he was in the ninth grade. Later he attended the prestigious Brown University and received a degree in applied math and economics.

"To make extra money I worked in restaurants, actually in this town. Food and restaurants were always of interest to me," said Simone. "I was a host, a busboy, a line chef, and a bartender."

While still at Brown University, Simone happened to pick up *World of Food* by Paula Wolfret. "I thought this woman was so knowledgeable and interesting," he remembers. "She had stories from the heart, about real people and culture. I bought the book and cooked every recipe in it."

From then on it was a quest and a hunger to know more about food culture and its history, especially Italian. Simone spent a month in Florence studying with author and teacher Giuliano Bugialli.

"While in Italy I met a bunch of people, learned to make pasta the right way, and experienced the real soul of Italian food," he said. "Later I had the exciting opportunity to go on several trips with the International Olive Oil Association. It was through one of these trips that I received a phone call; it was Paula Wolfret. It was a day before a large conference in Spain. (We had a mutual friend who told her about me.) She said she needed someone to help her make a squid ink risotto for 150 people and asked me if I was interested in helping her cook it. You cannot imagine what a thrill that was for me."

Back in Rhode Island in 2009, Simone opened The Sunnyside, a successful restaurant that achieved wonderful popularity. The Sunnyside only served breakfast and lunch and was located only 2 blocks down the street from his new location.

At the time I visited, Simone's had only been open for a little over a year. I asked what this building was before he took it over. "It was a rundown bar and restaurant that had not been performing for many years. My family and I bought the building. It took a long time to renovate it. It looked nothing like this!" he says.

Simone's now serves breakfast, lunch, and dinner, and they keep their food as close to their roots as possible. They also support the community by buying local and seasonal products and foods from the sea and the area.

THE ITALIAN LANGUAGE AMERICANIZED

In the interviews I was dealing with memories of what people f another generation. Many of the recipes' names were misspelled and were not the way they were spelled in Italy or any dictionary, for that matter. I realized this was because it was the way people thought they heard it. There is a round coffee cake or *ciambella*, meaning donut because it is usually made in a round ring. Then there's "*Brazadela*." My dear friend Mafalda "Muffie" Maiolini and the people in my small village spelled it "*Brasadella*" with and s instead of a z and two ls. Another spelling I found from Nelda Rossi was "*Bragalone*," all with very similar ingredients but different spellings.

I concluded that when the Italians came to this country the language changed and it became Americanized. They spoke it the way they heard it and spelled it the way they thought it should be spelled. "E" in Italian is pronounced as an "a," for example. Another example is *Tortellini* spelled *Tortallini*—the "e" changed to "a." There was also the slang and shortening of words—often the vowel at the end of a word is completed dropped and words like calamari are pronounced calamar and prosciutto is simple known as prociutt (sounds like "pro-shoot").

"A rose by any other name would smell as sweet" is a frequently-quoted line from William Shakespeare's play, *Romeo and Juliet*. Here Juliet seems to argue that it does not matter that Romeo is from her rival's house of Montague—that is, that he is named "Montague." The reference is often used to imply that the names of things do not effect what they really are. The play takes place in Verona, Italy!

TOMATO AND ROSEMARY RISOTTO

"My grandmother Edith Botta Simone loved this recipe," says Chef Joe Simone. "She is one of the only people I have met who stirs a jigger (or so) of wine into a finished risotto. She loved serving it with slow-cooked pork with braised leeks."

SERVES 4 AS A FIRST COURSE

3–4 cups mild chicken stock

2 tablespoons olive oil

½ cup finely chopped onion

1 heaping teaspoon minced fresh rosemary

1 cup Arborio, carnaroli, or other rice suitable for risotto

½ cup canned tomatoes with their juices, squeezed to a crush

2 tablespoons butter

3 tablespoons grated Parmigiano Reggiano

¼ cup dry white wine (optional)

Salt and pepper

Bring chicken stock to a boil in a saucepan, then slowly simmer on back burner.

In a large saucepan add olive oil and onions and cook for 3 to 4 minutes until they are wilted. Add rosemary and cook for 1 minute.

Add the rice and stir. Cook for 1 to 2 minutes until you can smell the rice.

Add 2 cups hot stock and turn down heat to low.

Cook slowly, stirring until the rice absorbs the stock.

Add more stock and repeat several times until the rice is approaching *al dente*. Add the tomatoes with the juice and cook for 3 to 4 minutes, adding more stock as needed until the rice has cooked.

Add butter and cheese, stir until well combined. Add wine, mixing again until well combined. Season with salt and pepper and serve with your choice of accompaniments.

CHEF'S TIP: Chopped tomatoes that come in a box work well in this recipe.

MARLENE BRIGIDA BALDWIN

Marlene Brigida Baldwin of Keene, New Hampshire, is the author of *Nonna's Cucina and Beyond: A Collection of Recipes and Anecdotes*, featuring Marlene's grandmother's Northern Italian recipes. I was served the same food as a child. Our grandparents came from the same region in Northern Italy, so we have a lot in common and we have had several delightful conversations about food, recipes, and the history of the area where she grew up, Plymouth, Massachusetts.

Marlene's grandparents came from poor backgrounds and circumstances in Italy, and like most Italians who immigrated to this country, they wanted a better life for themselves and their family. "Both my grandfathers, Angelo Cocchi and Tony Brigida, put family first and protected us all," Marlene said.

Her Italian families worked hard to be self-sufficient. She told me a story about how her grandmother, Agata Beccari Cocchi, would not let anything edible go to waste—even greens she found growing wild. "As a young girl, she would stop along the way home from work in the rice fields near Decima, in Northern Italy, to pick salad greens for dinner," Marlene said. "And my paternal grandmother, Liberal Mastroiorio Brigda, collected purslane and dandelions in her backyard, all her life."

"My grandparents, parents, and most of their siblings all had chickens and rabbits, large gardens, fruit trees, and the essential grape arbors for making wine. Angelo Cocchi, my grandfather, was known as the best wine maker in North Plymouth," Marlene said. "We still have his wine-making equipment and a few bottles of his last production in 1951, which probably has turned to vinegar."

In her grandmother's household, salad was served following the main course, Marlene recalled. And "Friday night was always spaghetti with tuna sauce or bean soup. Whatever the meal, it was always served with respect and with appreciation.

Marlene is the oldest member of the second generation in America. She has documented her family history through recipes and stories that help keep the Italian tradition and history alive.

TUNA SPAGHETTI

This dish was usually served for Friday night dinner at Marlene Brigida Baldwin's home when she was a child. It was also a favorite on Christmas Eve.

SERVES 4

¼–½ cup olive oil

1 yellow onion, chopped

¼–½ cup chopped fresh Italian parsley

Celery leaves or 1 stalk, minced

2 garlic cloves minced

2 (3-ounce) cans Italian tuna in olive oil

2 tablespoons tomato paste in 1 cup water

1 (8-ounce) can tomato sauce

Pepper to taste (Marlene suggests using a lot!)

1 pound angel hair pasta

Heat olive oil in a medium pan and sauté onion, parsley, and celery until translucent. Add garlic, being careful not to burn. Add all remaining ingredients except for the pasta and simmer for 10 to 15 minutes.

Boil pasta according to directions on package until *al dente*.

Drain pasta, place in a warm bowl, and toss with the sauce.

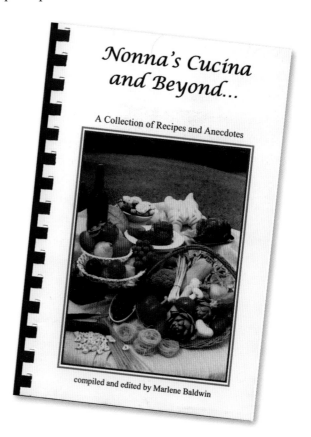

Nonna's Cucina and Beyond...

A Collection of Recipes and Anecdotes

compiled and edited by Marlene Baldwin

THE TORTELLINI PROJECT

As part of my research, I made a trip to Springfield, Massachusetts, where I met Rose Palazzi at an Italian coffee shop. She had just come from church.

"I used to attend Saint Anthony's," she said. "It was here in Agawam and in the Italian section, but it has since been closed." Rose and I talked for a long time and she invited me to her home where she gave me a cookbook and a video she made called *The Tortellini Project.*

"There was a large group of women who came from Saint Anne's Church in West Springfield, Springfield, and Agawam and surrounding communities to make tortellini, mostly around the holidays," she explained. "[We sold them] to benefit the church. They were a wonderful group of women." She went on to explain how everything was methodically done and well organized, from the day of buying the meats for the filling to drying, packing, and selling their product.

"The women would come in, sit at long tables; there were so many. They would sing and talk and only break for lunch, which consisted of nice Italian cold cuts, imported cheeses, and bread," Rose said. "Then it was back to work again. The church made money off these hard-working Italian women who did nothing but make tortellini." She went on to tell me people came from far and wide to purchase a bag containing 100 tortellini for $8.

Rose shared her recipe from the Bologna area of Northern Italy, where her husband's parents came from. I am publishing this recipe the way she described it to me.

ROSE PALAZZI'S TORTELLINI

SERVES 4-6

FILLING

1 pound ground pork

¼ pound mortadella, minced

2 eggs, slightly beaten

1 cup grated cheese

Pepper, to taste

1 teaspoon grated nutmeg

PASTA

2 cups of flour

3 eggs

½ eggshell of olive oil or water

FOR THE FILLING

Pan fry the pork for a short time, add the mortadella, then let cool. Place in a bowl and add eggs, cheese, pepper, and nutmeg. Combine until mixed well.

FOR THE PASTA

Place all ingredients in a food processor and mix.

Put the pasta through a pasta machine to desired thickness (Rose likes it thin), cut in squares, fill with filling, and twist.

ROSE SAYS: "I put the finished tortellini in the freezer immediately. When frozen, I place them in ziplock bags and freeze until ready to cook."

Alba Papi's "batticarne"(meat pounder) and mine bought in Italy.

PRIMI

Meat, Poultry & Seafood

BAKED STUFFED LOBSTER

When I was growing up in Sagamore Village, there used to be a rotary just over the bridge. Just off the circle was Eleanor's Restaurant, started by Eleanor Sorenti Reggiani and her husband Charlie. Charlie was the bartender from 1936 until the 1960s. They were famous for their Baked Stuffed Lobster.

SERVES 1

1 (2½- or 3-pound) lobster

6 tablespoons butter, melted

2 tablespoons lemon juice

FOR THE STUFFING
(PER LOBSTER)
¼ cup minced scallops

1 tablespoon dry sherry

1 tablespoon lemon juice

1 teaspoon fresh chopped thyme

1 cup Ritz cracker crumbs

¼ cup potato chips, crushed

3 tablespoons of butter or a bit more if you'd like

Fresh ground pepper to taste

1 large lettuce leaf

Prepare lobster (you can find instructions online or your fishmonger can do it for you)

Preheat the oven to 400°F.

Combine melted butter and lemon juice; set aside

FOR THE STUFFING

In a bowl, mix the scallops, sherry, lemon juice, and thyme.

Add the cracker crumbs, potato chips, 3 tablespoons butter, and pepper to taste.

Toss gently, mixing well and set aside.

With the lobster on its back on a baking pan, sprinkle lobster cavity with freshly ground pepper, then brush the lobster with 2 tablespoons lemon butter.

Lightly fill the cavity with the stuffing. Drizzle with remaining lemon butter.

Insert a long wooden skewer through the tail and into the body. This will prevent the tail from curling. Cover with the lettuce leaf for the first 10 minutes to keep the stuffing moist and prevent it from over cooking.

Bake for 25 to 35 minutes total.

JAMES DIBIASE

After more than a century in America, how does a family preserve its Italian heritage?

For the DiBiase family, the answer is two-fold: through the family customs and cooking, and through a website documenting their ancestors' arrivals in Maine.

I visited James DiBiase and his wife Francesca DiMillo DiBiase in their home in Portland, Maine, where James is the director of the Italian Heritage Center. This is a group committed to preserving and promoting the Italian heritage, culture, and history in America.

Like many Italians fleeing the poverty of Southern Italy, James's father, Giacomo DiBiase, came to America in 1901 or 1902 when he was just 16.

Born in 1885, he was, like his father, a stonecutter. Giacomo was from Letto-manopello, in the region of Abruzzo, the province of Pescara. He would go up into the mountains to work on stones. "All they had to eat was a loaf of Italian bread with tomatoes and olive oil," James explained.

In America, Giacomo settled in Stonington, Maine, where he worked in the quarries. After his wife Rosaria died in 1925, he returned to Italy and married again, this time choosing Rosaria's cousin Rosina as his wife. Giacomo and Rosina became the parents of five children. Giacomo and Rosina ran a grocery store for 24 years while Giacomo worked full-time as a crane and derrick operator at the Portland Company. He died in 1971.

James was born in Munjoy Hill in Portland. While the area at the bottom of the hill was Italian, James and his family lived on the top of hill in an ethnically mixed neighborhood. After James and Fran married, James worked as a mechanical engineer while Fran did temporary work and raised their five children. It is their daughter who has established the website outlining her family's history, starting with the birth of her grandfather Giacomo.

Preserving a heritage is always a challenging task, even in a household where Fran, who does most of the cooking, bakes wonderful *pizzelles*, Italian cookies, and cowjunes, a deep-fried delicacy stuffed with chocolate, chick peas, and orange.

"We, as part of the Italian culture, have become all the dreamers, wishers, prayers, and so forth of yesteryear," Fran said. "As we age, we are losing it, and our children are not becoming like us. The difficulties were very trying as we were growing up, but we survived it. And all that we have been taught, our children have our history to talk about, but the interest it not there. They are Americans now."

BRACIOLA

The following is a recipe from Luigi and Maria DiMillo, which was given to me by Francisca. There are two ways to cook and serve this braciola. One is sliced and served by itself, the other is to serve it sliced over spaghetti.

SERVES 6–8

2 pounds top round or flank steak, pounded thin

Salt and pepper to taste

4 thin slices of salt pork, salami, or prosciutto

3 eggs, hard-boiled and sliced

Orange skins, sliced thin

Onions, sliced thin

2 tablespoons chopped garlic

1 cup chopped fresh Italian parsley

½ cup fresh chopped basil

Romano cheese, grated

¼ cup olive oil

½ cup white wine

3 cups favorite tomato sauce

Sprinkle steaks with salt and pepper. Then layer pork, salami, or prosciutto; egg slices; orange skins; onions; garlic; parsley; basil; and cheese evenly over the steaks, roll them up, and tie them securely with string.

Heat olive oil in a large sauté pan, and brown the steak rolls, turning for even color.

Add white wine and tomato sauce, cover, and simmer for about 2 hours until meat is tender. Serve as you wish.

STEAK AND OIL

This was our unromantic family name for a dish my Grandmother Carafoli use to make for my grandfather. It was one of his favorite meals. A glass of his homemade red wine, a salad of bitter greens, and a piece of our local "horn" bread from Louis Market were all that was needed to make him happy.

The secret of this recipe is to work fast! Also, be sure you use a heavy skillet (to hold the heat) with a really tight-fitting lid. It is one of those dishes that works best when made for one or two people.

SERVES 1

1 small (8 ounces) fillet of beef

1–2 cloves of garlic

1 tablespoon of olive oil

Salt and pepper to taste

3 tablespoons of cold water

Cut a small fillet of beef (about 8 ounces) into small cubes (about ¼ inch) and set aside on a plate. Coarsely chop 1 or 2 cloves of garlic and set them aside too.

Pour a thin film of oil into a medium-sized cast-iron skillet and set it over high heat. Add the garlic and cook until it starts to turn light brown. The oil must be extremely hot, but don't wait until the garlic scorches! Quickly add the meat; shaking the skillet, toss rapidly with a spatula to stir-fry for about 30 seconds. Add salt and pepper to taste and 3 tablespoons cold water. Cover the skillet immediately, remove from heat, and let it rest for 2–3 minutes. This helps release the juices from the meat, making a wonderful sauce to be sopped up with good Italian bread.

"We lived over Louie's Market in Sagamore and that is where I was born. My mother told me I was born at seven o'clock in the morning while outside many of the men who worked at Keith Car Works were walking Adams Street harmonizing Italian songs on their way to work. My father, Augustus Ansaloni was down in the basement of the house, below the store, baking the famous "horn bread." That is why I like bread and I like music!"

—GENEVIEVE ANSALONI MOONEY, 1995

CLASSIC ITALIAN MEATBALLS

This is a basic recipe for Italian-American meatballs. You can add other ingredients such as a few pieces of mortadella or a dash of nutmeg for variety.

MAKES 12-15 MEATBALLS

1 tablespoon butter

1 small onion, minced

1½ pounds ground beef

½ pound ground pork

1 egg, lightly beaten

¼ cup breadcrumbs

¼ cup whole milk

1 tablespoon chopped fresh Italian parsley

1 garlic clove, minced

¼ cup grated Parmigiano Reggiano cheese

Salt and freshly ground pepper

¼ cup all-purpose flour

Olive oil for frying

Heat butter in small sauté pan. Add onion and sauté until lightly brown.

Place all the ingredients, except the flour and olive oil, in a large mixing bowl, add cooked onions, and mix with your hands until well combined.

Roll meat mixture into balls smaller than golf balls.

Roll in the flour and set aside.

In a large skillet heat a small amount of oil over medium heat. When hot, add the meatballs and brown on all sides.

Put your marinara sauce in a saucepan, heat and arrange the meatballs in the sauce and cook for 1 to 2 hours until done.

LAMB AND EGGPLANT MEATBALLS IN SIMPLE TOMATO SAUCE

Julia Della Croce developed this recipe. She explains: "I added the eggplant to the meatballs because it gives you less meat and also makes the meatball more tender. What is more classic than mixing meat and eggplant?"

MAKES 20 MEATBALLS

1 medium eggplant

1 cup day-old sturdy bread, such as sourdough or country loaf, crusts removed, cut into ¼-inch cubes (2 ounces trimmed weight)

1 egg

1 scant teaspoon fine sea salt

½ teaspoon freshly ground black or white pepper

1 large clove garlic, minced

1 pound ground lamb leg or shoulder

3 tablespoons minced fresh Italian parsley

2 tablespoons fresh minced rosemary or 2 teaspoons dried crushed rosemary

Extra-virgin or pure olive oil for frying

2 cups homemade meatless tomato sauce of your choice

Preheat an oven to 400°F.

Prick the eggplant in several places with a cake tester or sharp knife. Place it on a baking sheet and roast until entirely collapsed, soft, and charred, about 35 minutes.

Meanwhile, place bread cubes in a shallow soup bowl and cover with water. Soak until moistened, several minutes. Drain and squeeze excess water from bread.

When the eggplant is cool enough to handle, push out excess seeds. (Leaving some of them in with the pulp adds texture to the meatball.) Chop the pulp finely in a food processor. Transfer it to a sieve and press with a spoon to drain off excess liquid.

In an ample mixing bowl, whisk together egg, sea salt, pepper, and garlic. Stir in the prepared bread cubes. Use your hands to break them up until they are well blended with the egg mixture. Add the chopped eggplant, ground lamb, parsley, and rosemary. Using your fingers, mix the ingredients together without overworking them. If you have time, chill the mixture before forming the meatballs; this step can help you shape it into perfectly round spheres, but it is not essential.

With wet hands, form the mixture into equally sized balls about 1¼ inches in diameter, no larger than golf balls.

Prepare a platter with two layers of paper towels next to the burner over which you will be cooking.

Recipe continues on page 132

In an ample skillet or frying pan, pour enough olive oil to cover the bottom of the pan and warm it over medium heat. Fry the meatballs in batches to avoid overcrowding; there should be plenty of room around each for proper searing. When they have developed a light crust and look golden brown, about 10 minutes, transfer them to the paper towels to drain. If necessary, drain off smoky oil and add fresh oil to the pan to prevent the bits that settle on the bottom from burning. Warm the oil once again and finish frying.

If you are serving the meatballs in tomato sauce, warm the sauce over medium heat and slip the browned meatballs into it. Cook them through, about 20 minutes. Serve at once. If you plan to make the meatballs in advance, cool and store them, with or without the tomato sauce, in a covered storage container in the refrigerator for up to 4 days. Alternatively, freeze them for up to 3 months.

COOK'S TIP: Another option for meatballs is using the ingredients from La Civetta's Chef Fabio Pozzati's Polpettone (see recipe page *143).*

SPAGHETTI AND MEATBALLS

In most Italian restaurants in America, what stands out on the menu is spaghetti and meatballs. It is probably one of the best comfort foods. The American bowl of spaghetti topped off with several meatballs in a pool of red sauce and sprinkled with Parmigiano Reggiano cheese echo what most Americans think of as "Italian cuisine," that is, unless you are Italian.

If you go to Italy looking for spaghetti and meatballs, you would probably only find it on a menu catering to Americans.

Yes, there are meatballs in Italy but not the same as those we have in America.

Each region in Italy has its own version called *polpette*. They usually consist of a mixture of beef and pork (sometimes they are just beef), onions, breadcrumbs or bread soaked in milk, egg, parsley, and Parmigiano Reggiano cheese. *Polpette* can be made from other meats, such as turkey, veal, chicken, even fish. Some are eaten plain as a meal, and sometimes you'll find them in a soup. Chances are, though, you'll find them made by the home cook rather than in most restaurants.

The origin of spaghetti and meatballs started with Italian immigrants coming to America between 1880 and 1920. Here, they found the food available to them unfamiliar and they needed to improvise. Along with canned tomatoes, the immigrants used ingredients that were readily available to them to make dishes that tasted like home. The Italian cuisine became a blend of Italian and American. The marinara sauce we all know and love, or "sailor's sauce," originated in Naples. *Marinaro* means sailor.

Italian immigrants used many other ingredients and seasonings as they were assimilated into American culture. It's all delicious, and most of it very different from what you might find in Italy. Here, on pages 128, 131-132, and 143 are several versions of meatballs, you choose your favorite.

LOBSTER CACCIATORA

This recipe is a dish my great uncle made when he came to visit us when I was very young. I have recreated it through memory.

Cacciatora is Italian for hunter. Hunters' stews usually refer to stews made with fresh rabbit, poultry, and game. The game off the shores of Cape Cod is lobster, fish, and shellfish. I pick my own mussels and dig for clams off the beach near my home. I am also fortunate to know many local fishermen who offer me their fresh catches of the day. With all of this abundance of local fish and shellfish available to me, I created this *cacciatore*-style dish very close to the flavors of the dish Zio Cherubino, my grandfather's brother and a chef from Connecticut made for the family when he and his wife Tersilla visited us.

MAKES 4 SERVINGS

FOR THE SAUCE

4 tablespoons olive oil

1 clove garlic, minced

1 Italian red finger pepper or ¼ teaspoon red pepper flakes. More may be added for a hotter sauce.

1 can (28-ounce) peeled crushed tomatoes

1 tablespoon chopped basil

1 teaspoon chopped oregano

4 tablespoons chopped fresh Italian parsley

1 dried bay leaf

Salt to taste

1 pint lobster or clam stock (optional)

FOR THE LOBSTERS

2 (1½- or 2-pound) live lobsters

2 tablespoons clarified butter

2 tablespoons olive oil

2 tablespoons cognac

1 cup dry white wine

One recipe for *polenta* (page 81)

FOR THE SAUCE

Heat olive oil in a medium saucepan. Add garlic and red pepper or pepper flakes, cook until garlic is slightly browned (do not burn it).

Add and stir in the tomatoes, fresh herbs, and salt. Add 1 pint lobster or clam stock to the sauce at this point. Simmer until thickened, about 30 minutes. During the last five minutes, prepare and cook the lobsters.

COOK'S TIP: Clam juice may also be added if stock is not available.

FOR THE LOBSTERS

If you are timid about killing a lobster, have your fishmonger do it for you.

Melt butter in a large, deep skillet. Add olive oil and turn up the heat to high. At this point, everything should be done very quickly. Add the lobsters in the shell, and sear them on all sides. Pour on the cognac and ignite it.

Add the wine and the sauce, reduce the heat, and cover. Simmer for 20 minutes. Serve with a large slice of *polenta*.

COOK'S TIP: I always use fresh herbs for cooking, and they are especially important in this dish. But if you must use dried herbs, use about ⅓ the amount specified.

COOK'S TIP: To turn this into a great stew, add a handful of mussels, clams, squid, or pieces of white fish.

TONY'S COLONIAL FOOD

313 Atwell Ave.
Providence, RI 02903
(401) 621-8675
tonyscolonial.com

Antonio DiCicco owns Tony's Colonial Food and has been providing shoppers with the finest imported and domestic Italian foods since 1952. It is a place known for its quality meats and cheeses, extensive selection of imported olive oils and vinegars, antipasti, and other specialties like imported porcini mushrooms, Italian candies, confections, prepared foods, and tasty homemade sausage, mild and hot. Tony has one of the largest selections of imported and homemade pastas in Rhode Island. He supplies many local chefs with his products, especially the pasta.

"I came to this country from Lazio outside of Rome," says Tony. "Where we lived we had a big church on a mountain: *chiesa di montagna*." He explains how, during the war, the Germans hid inside the church. To get them out the Americans had to destroy the church and in doing so the whole town was destroyed. "After the war, we all had to live in tents," says Tony. "We were refugees and I was one of them."

Tony came to America in 1955 and started working in this store as an employee. "It was 1958 and I was 21," he remembers. "The owner was close to 60 and I worked for him for five or six years. Then he wanted to sell it. That is when I took it over. At that time, it was a very small 900-foot variety store, now it is 3,000."

PAN-ROASTED SAUSAGE AND GRAPES

SERVES 2

2 tablespoons olive oil, more for drizzling

1 pound mild or hot lean sausage, cut into 2-inch pieces

2 cups sliced seedless grapes

Salt and pepper, to taste

1 sprig fresh rosemary

Heat olive oil in heavy skillet over medium heat.

Add sausage and sear on both sides. If the sausage renders a lot of fat, drain it off.

Turn off the heat and add grapes on top of the sausage, sprinkle with olive oil, salt, pepper, and fresh rosemary. Cover and cook on medium heat for 15 to 20 minutes, stirring occasionally.

Serve as a main course with Julia della Croce's recipe for Broccoli Rabe Pesto served with boiled potatoes (page 58).

COOK'S TIP: Gasbarro's Chianti Classico Riserva is a great wine selection to accompany this dish.

GASBARRO'S WINES

361 Atwells Ave., Providence, RI 02903, 401-421-4170

gasbarros.com

Up the street on Atwells Avenue, after you leave all the restaurants and shops, you find one of the oldest and finest Italian wine shops in New England. Gasbarro's Wines. In business since 1898, Gasbarro's was one of the first wine shops to import wines from Italy and distribute them around New England. Before moving to their current location in 1973, the store used to be located across the street from St. John's Catholic Church. In those days the bishop was extremely powerful when it came to business dealings, and he wasn't too keen on having a wine distributor so close to his church. Antonio Gasbarro was told they he would not be approved for a business license unless he blocked the windows and made the entrance on the side of the building. Being brought up in an Italian-Catholic family, a member of the church, and a good businessman, Antonio complied with the bishop's demands and received his license.

He ran the business with his oldest son Ugo and his other nine children, four girls and five boys, who all worked in the store for several decades.

In the late 1960s, Ugo's son Lombard took over the store and ran it until he passed away in 1981. Continuing in his family's footsteps Lombard's son Mark, who began working in the store at the age of 16, continues to build the legacy of premium fine wines. Today Gasbarro's is recognized as one of the top retailers of Italian wine in the country.

OSTERIA LA CIVETTA

133 Main St.
Falmouth, MA 02540
(508) 540-1616

Restaurateurs Alberto Toselli and his wife Giovanna Tassinari were both born in the small town of Cento in the Emilia-Romagna region of northern Italy, the same region where my grandfather was born.

They built a house on Cape Cod in the early 1990s, and for many years traveled back and forth between Cape Cod and Italy. About a decade later, after their daughter Sara graduated from college in Bologna, they decided to open an authentic Italian restaurant in Falmouth.

"There was already another one here at the time. It's Italian-American," Alberto said. "So—totally different concept idea, almost a near opposite, the Italian-American compared to the Italian."

Alberto described the differences between the Italian and Italian-American cuisines. When Italian immigrants arrived, he said, they tried to replicate the food they ate back home, but they were unable to obtain authentic ingredients. "They had to adjust those, kind of compromise, and so your mother or grandmother had to do the food with what was available," Alberto said. Children growing up in Italian families believed they were eating Italian food, whereas it was Italian-American food. In contrast, today "you can have whatever you like coming from Italy," Alberto claims. So now it is possible to run an authentic Italian restaurant in America.

Alberto and Giovanna heard about a building for rent on Main Street in Falmouth. Alberto remembers that when he called the landlord to inquire about the building, the landlord said, "It's a shoe box." To which Alberto responded, "Oh, it's perfect, perfect."

And so in this building they created their Italian osteria. The closest English translation for osteria is tavern—a casual place serving great food. From Italy, they shipped a container with the tables, furniture, ceramics, and everything else they needed to furnish their genuine Italian osteria. Much of the furniture came from old farmhouses and flea markets, and was chosen to create a warm, friendly ambience. Osteria la Civetta, which means The Little Owl Tavern, opened its doors on October 4, 2007.

"We were scared the first day," Alberto recalled. "We didn't know how it would work and it was a Friday. We opened the door. No grand opening. No soft opening. Nothing like that. And here we are, eight years later."

Along the way, Alberto learned many things about running a restaurant on Cape Cod. "Nowadays here it's all about farm-to-table, changing menus, stuff like that," he said. "Back then, I got in touch with the farmer because for us it's so natural. It's natural as an Italian to get in touch with the farmer, the butcher there, fish, fishing boats, something like that." But when Alberto spoke to the man on the fishing boat, he learned things aren't done that way here. The farmer's reaction was more extreme. "He looked at me like I was an alien from Mars," Alberto said. "He said, 'You have the distributor inside, why you should come to me to get the fresh vegetables and stuff like that?' He didn't understand me. Again, nowadays it's pretty common. Farm to table."

Some patrons were confused because the menu at Osteria la Civetta changed according to the seasons. "They come, they get their food, come back two or three months later and ask for the same food, it's not there," said Alberto. The customers will reply, "What? We came here just for this." But that's okay with Alberto, who says. "You have to tell them, educate them little by little."

Another difference between an Italian restaurant and an American restaurant is that in Italy the chef goes to the market and then designs his menu. In America, Alberto said, it's the opposite—what the chef buys is determined by the pre-determined menu. "I'm going to do this, this, this. And then you call the distributor."

At Osteria la Civetta, Alberto serves the food of his native Emilia-Romagna region, one of Italy's 19 distinct regions, each with its own cuisine. The area is a gastronome's delight and the birthplace of many delicious foods, such as prosciutto, mortadella, Aceto Balsmico, and Parmigiano Reggiano. The soil is good for pumpkins, "so we make tortelloni with pumpkins because we are next to the Po River," Alberto said.

Since opening in 2007, Alberto added a second dining room and a small bar. The restaurant now seats 80. Each day the chefs make fresh pasta by hand, using free-range eggs. The restaurant incorporates daily specials into an authentic Italian cuisine that is "simple, honest, and unpretentious."

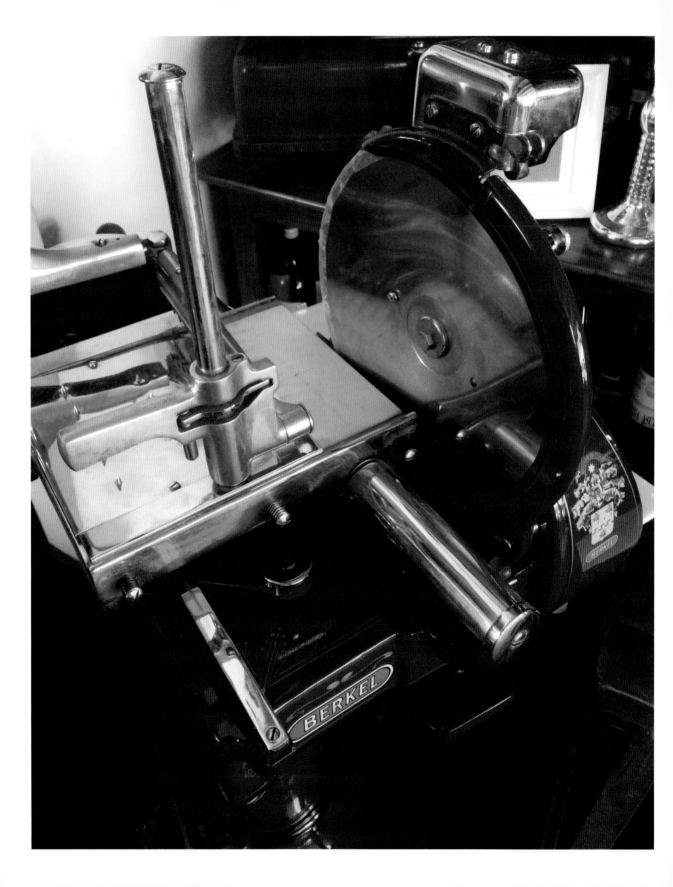

POLPETTONE

This recipe for polpettone is from Osteria la Civetta's Chef Fabio Pozzati's. It is typically Italian. Pozzati is from the region of Ferrara, Italy.

SERVES 6-8

1 cup bread crumbs

¼ cup milk

1 pound ground beef

1 pound ground pork

¾ cup ground prosciutto crudo

¼ cup grated Parmigiano Reggiano

1 cup ground mortadella

½ cup chopped fresh Italian parsley

1 small onion, minced

¼ teaspoon ground nutmeg, or to taste

2 eggs, slightly beaten

Salt and pepper, to taste

Soften the breadcrumbs with the milk. Once they are soft, squeeze them well, and add to bowl with all the remaining ingredients. With your hands, mix everything together until well incorporated.

To give the polpettone its shape, place it on a piece of parchment paper and roll the paper over it to form a large log. Tightly twist the ends closed and place log in the refrigerator to rest for at least an hour. (If desired, divide the mixture in two and freeze one for later.)

There are two ways to cook the polpettone: It can be poached in broth or baked in the oven at 350°F until the internal temperature reaches 165°F.

Serve with boiled or roasted potatoes.

ANTONELLI'S POULTRY

Chris Morris, owner
62 De Pasquale Ave.
Providence RI 02903
(401) 421-8739

Antonelli's Poultry has been in business since 1853 and is the only live poultry store in Rhode Island. It is the real thing! In the store you will find a glass chest with freshly slaughtered whole chickens, their parts, special orders, plus chicken and duck eggs. Opposite the main door at the back of the store is a thick plastic curtain. I pushed it aside and walked into a room with an intense, overpowering odor. What did I expect walking into a room full of cages, with pigeons, chickens, ducks and rabbits? In the middle of the room several butchers were standing in front of stainless steel tables with knives slaughtering, cleaning, and preparing the poultry. While I was there, one gentleman waited and watched the process. I watched him as he carried his freshly slaughtered, still warm chicken out of the store in a plastic bag. If you want to see where your food comes from, this is the place. It is an Old World establishment that still attracts many immigrants, not only the Italians but Chinese, Japanese, Cambodian, Jews, and Irish who come to live in Rhode Island. I had a chance to ask Chris Morris how he became owner of Antonelli's.

"When my father-in-law, Frank Antonelli, owner of the store, became ill, he asked if I could watch the store for a while until he could sell it, I said yeah. In a short time I got to know the business, and realized this is pretty easy to run; I mean, a customer comes in, wants to buy a chicken, you sell it, and they're gone. That was pretty much the way it went."

Chris left a high-paying, union job in construction to watch the store for his father in law. "My union boss called me and asked if I was coming back," remembers Chris. "I said no, I think I want to run the chicken store." He's been doing just that since 1975.

When Chris took over the store, they were only selling chickens. Now he has expanded to ducks, rabbits, pheasants, quail, geese, and partridge.

CHICKEN UNDER A BRICK

This is a simple, delicious, and easy way to cook chicken with an Italian touch using *Cunsa* (see recipe on page xvii) instead of just salt and pepper for seasoning while getting the rest of the meal together. This is a wonderful dish to serve with sauteed broccoli rabe.

SERVES 4

1 2 ½- to 3- pound chicken, backbone removed

3 tablespoon olive oil

Kosher salt, freshly ground pepper or *Cunsa* (pg. xvii)

1 brick wrapped in foil

Large iron skillet

Place chicken on a work surface, skin side up. Using you palms, press firmly on the breastbone to flatten the breast.

Rub chicken with oil and season with salt and pepper or *Cunsa*.

Tuck wings slightly under breast.

Heat the skillet over high heat until hot and place the chicken skin side down in the skillet. Set the brick on top, reduce heat to medium-high and cook until the skin is golden brown and crisp, about 15 to 20 minutes.

Remove brick, and, using tongs, turn the chicken so the skin side is up. Replace brick and continue cooking until chicken is cooked through and when a thermometer inserted into the thickest part of thigh registers 165°F.

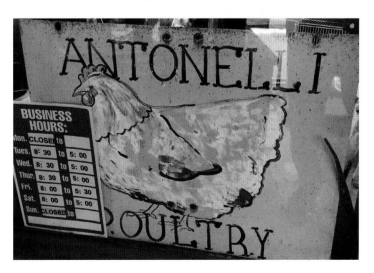

D&D MARKET

276 Franklin Ave.
Hartford, CT 06114
(860) 296-3261
danddmarket.com

D&D Market in Hartford's Little Italy got its start after a disagreement over a bottle of milk. Back in the 1920s, Daniel D'Aprile's grandfather, Vito D'Aprile, was working as general manager of a chain of six or eight ethnic grocery stores. "One day a lady came in and broke a gallon of milk on the floor," Daniel explained. "In those days, the gallons of milk were in glass." He goes on to explain that his grandfather told the woman to not worry that he would clean up the milk. However, Daniel recalled, the son of the owner called Vito over and said, "'You're going to charge for that milk, right?'

"My grandfather says, 'No, I'm not going to charge her for that milk. She's a good customer.' The son said, 'Vito, if you don't charge her for that milk, I don't think you're going to be working here,' and Vito said, 'You know what? If I got to charge her for that milk, I don't want to work here.'"

Vito opened his own store and put his previous employer out of business in one year. "My grandfather survived, and he thrived," Daniel said. "That's how D&D came to be—over one gallon of milk. Can you believe that? Crazy as it sounds."

Daniel is now the third generation of D'Apriles working at the store.

Vito came from Bari, Italy, when he was 16. He first went to work in the tobacco fields of Windsor Locks, Connectiut. "He worked his tail off, and he worked his way up the ladder a little bit, and he leased some land," Daniel said. In the 1920s Vito had a tremendous tobacco crop, which was then wiped out by a hailstorm, and he lost his entire investment in an hour. That was the end of Vito's career as a tobacco farmer, and he fortuitously went into the grocery business.

Vito's son Achille "Kelly" D'Aprile joined Vito in the store full-time in 1959. Two years later, the store moved to a larger location on Franklin Avenue. Daniel joined his father and grandfather in the store in the early 1980s, after he graduated from college. By the mid-1990s Daniel was running the store's daily operations in a larger, updated store. Daniel's children Lisa and Daniel work at the store on holidays and weekends—they represent the fourth generation of D'Apriles at the store.

The store offers many Italian butcher shop specialties, including pork brasci-oles, meatballs, and veal dishes. It sells cheeses such as stracchino, robiola, caprino, caciocavallo, and many more. It offers specialty items such as octopus salad and over a dozen varieties of imported olives. The market also offers many prepared Italian dishes and holds food events.

"The core of this business is Italian specialty foods," Daniel said. "That's the way we started, and it's the way we're continuing. Italian specialty foods."

D&D recently expanded into a second store at 675 Wolcott Hill Road in Wethersfield. Today, the market's motto remains the same as always: A piece of Italy in Hartford.

Vito and wife Anna.

D&D MARKET'S AND THE D'APRILE FAMILY'S ROASTED BACCALÀ SALAD

"An Italian Christmas Eve tradition at our home. Enjoy!"—Danny D'Aprile

SERVES 6-8

1-2 pounds *baccalà* or 3-4 pounds already soaked cod

1 large jar *Giardiniera* (pickled vegetables) or 2 small jars, rinsed well and drained

1 clove garlic, sliced

1 teaspoon course black pepper

¼–½ cup extra-virgin olive oil

2-3 tablespoons chopped Italian parsley

Prepare the cod by soaking it: see tip below.

Place the *baccalà* on a baking sheet.

On the upper rack of your oven broil both sides of the fish until there is a nice golden color all around it and the fish is cooked through.

Remove from rack and break the fish into pieces (bite sized) into a bowl.

Add *giardiniera*, garlic, black pepper, and olive oil. Add just enough oil so the result is not too oily.

Toss well and place in a serving dish, garnish with parsley. This can be served warm, room temperature, or cold as a small side.

COOK'S TIP: *Baccalà* is dried salted codfish, so it needs to be soaked in water for 2 to 3 days, with the water being changed frequently to remove the salt and prepare for cooking. An alternative is to purchase already soaked *baccalà*. Some Italian specialty grocers, like D&D Market, sell *baccalà* which has been soaked. It simply needs to be rinsed well and patted dry with paper towels before using it in a recipe.

VEAL SALTIMBOCCA

This is the D'Aprile family's recipe for Veal Saltimbocca. It's the recipe they use to prepare the dish that they sell at D&D Market if you prefer that they do the cooking for you. The D'Aprile's hope you enjoy their Veal Saltimbocca as much as their family does!

SERVES 6-8

1⅓ pounds veal cutlets (chicken, beef, or pork cutlets can be substituted)

Salt and pepper to taste

¼ pound prosciutto di Parma, thinly sliced

Fresh sage leaves

¼ cup extra-virgin olive oil

4 tablespoons butter

1 cup white wine

½ lemon (juiced)

Season cutlets with salt and pepper.

Layer half of the cutlets with 1 slice of prosciutto, folded to to cover the top of the cutlet.

Place 1 whole sage leaf on top of the prosciutto, then place another piece of veal on top of the sage leaf. Continue until all the veal is used.

The cutlets should be pounded to help them hold their shape, otherwise they will not be easy to flip. Some people tie them or use toothpicks, which is not desireable.

Heat a large skillet over medium heat.

Heat 2 tablespoons extra-virgin olive oil and 1 tablespoon butter in a pan and sauté half the veal for 2 to 3 minutes on one side; flip and sauté an additional 1 to 2 minutes until they are cooked enough. Transfer to warm plate and repeat with remaining veal, adding additional oil and butter as needed.

Transfer the last of the cooked veal to the warm platter and return pan to heat.

Reduce heat to medium low, add wine, and scrape pan drippings with wine. Add lemon juice and remaining 2 tablespoons butter to the pan. Pour pan juices over the veal and serve. Veal can be rolled or served flat, as the D'Apriles do.

SHIRLEY'S SAUSAGE

Shirley Pagliarani and her husband, Joseph (Paddy) ran the Sagamore Inn on Cape Cod for 45 years. Her cooking became famous locally. She would start cooking early in the morning, seven days a week, making 40 quarts of spaghetti sauce, 8 gallons of clam chowder, her special red clam sauce, 45 pounds of pot roast with her "bodacious" gravy, and her well-known sausage patties. Paddy has passed away and the restaurant was sold to local residents, Michael and Suzanne Bilodeau, but some of Shirley's famous recipes are still served today. In fact, Shirley herself is a regular at the new place. Shirley made batches of this recipe for homemade sausage with not less than 10 pounds of meat at a time! But don't worry, I've adjusted it for a smaller crowd.

6 cloves garlic

2 cups dry white wine (and a little to drink)

2 pounds ground pork shoulder

1½ teaspoons salt

Lots of freshly ground pepper

Crush the garlic and wrap in a small piece of cheesecloth, tying tightly. Place wrapped garlic in the wine and macerate overnight in the refrigerator.

The next day, combine pork, salt, and pepper in a large bowl, adding the wine a little at a time so the meat is moist but not wet. Shape into patties and use in spaghetti sauce or as a side with pasta. It's also great as a breakfast sausage served with a fried egg, or crumbled and put on a pizza.

FRIGO'S GOURMET FOODS

90 William St.
Springfield, MA 01105
(413) 732-5428
frigofoods.com

Frigo's Gourmet Foods started when five brothers from the small northern Italian town of Dolo, in the province of Venice, in the region of Veneto, wanted the American dream. In Italy they were cheesemakers and, with their recipes in hand for mozzarella, provolone, asiago, and fontina, they came to the United States and went directly to Wisconsin in pursuit of that dream. Why Wisconsin?

"Wisconsin was a big dairy state," explains Amadeo Frigo's grandson Joseph Amadeo Frigo. "The air was good and had the three seasons to age the cheese. Back in those days they didn't have a lot of refrigeration, so they needed the three seasons to age the different cheeses."

Later, two of the brothers, Stefano and Amadeo, came to the east coast. Their brothers in the mid-west made the cheese and shipped it to them. Joe said they made a good living selling the Italians in Springfield their favorite cheeses. The original market on Williams Street started in 1950 and has been in business ever since.

During this time, Joe's father came out of the service and, with the help of the GI Bill, attended meat-cutting school. He learned how to slaughter pigs and cattle, prepare cuts of veal and pork, and make his own signature sausage, which was a great addition to the store's cheeses and other products.

Joe joined the business, too. "When I got out of college in the late 1980s I took over the business. It was at a time when prepared food started to be a big item," he said. "We broke down walls, added a real kitchen, and started making our own prepared foods like eggplant Parmesan, stuffed pork chops, salads, and sandwiches. We also now have a catering service, make gift baskets, and the like."

Because the business was so successful, the company opened a second store in East Longmeadow, Massachusetts, in 2005.

"I am old school," Joe went on to say. "I've always wanted the store to keep an Old World feel and carry products my grandfather carried, but still have a nice selection of prepared foods. I'm keeping up with the trends, so to speak. I am very proud that I am the third generation and I am still able to keep that tradition going."

Joe, Renzo and Amedo Frigo.

STUFFED PORK CHOPS WITH MARSALA SAUCE

¾ cup dry breadcrumbs

¼ cup Parmigiano Reggiano grated

¼ cup mozzarella cheese, shredded

2 cloves minced garlic

4 slices of prosciutto

¼ teaspoon ground fennel

2 tablespoons chopped fresh Italian parsley

White wine

Olive oil

4 (1½-inch-thick) center-cut pork chops

Preheat oven to 375°F.

In a small bowl mix the breadcrumbs, Parmigiano Reggiano, mozzarella, garlic, prosciutto, fennel, and parsley. Moisten with white wine and olive oil, just until mixture holds together.

Using a sharp knife, create a pocket in the pork chop by making a horizontal cut through the center. Do not cut all the way through.

Stuff the pork chop with prepared mixture.

Brown pork chops in olive oil about 5 minutes per side. Place pork chops in a baking dish and cover with Marsala sauce. Bake for 30 to 45 minutes.

MARSALA SAUCE

SAUCE FOR 4 SERVINGS

3 tablespoons olive oil

1 tablespoon butter

½ pound mushrooms, sliced

2 cloves garlic, minced

½ cup Marsala wine

2 tablespoons flour

1 cup water or chicken broth

Salt and pepper to taste

Heat the oil and butter in a sauté pan. Add the garlic and cook for 1 minute. Add the mushrooms and sauté for 5–10 minutes until slightly browned. Add Marsala and bring to a boil.

Stir water or broth together with the flour to make a roux. Strain to remove any lumps from the mixture, then pour it into the mushrooms. Heat and stir

SULMONA MEAT MARKET

32 A Parmenter St., Boston, MA
(617) 742-2791

Sulmona Meat Market, owned by Domonico and son Franco, is one of the oldest businesses in the area. They sell homemade sausages year-round, and during the holidays you'll find *zampone* and *cotechino*, traditional recipes from Modena dating back to the 1500s.

One fan who has just moved to the North End says this place is a "Throwback to the 1960s . . . the good, friendly, consistently fresh neighborhood butcher is rare these days . . . with box-sized grocery stores, chain markets, etc., many of the good ones have been pushed out. Sulmona is great—you won't find refrigerated meat cases here because everything is cut to order. I moved here to the North End a year ago, and this is my go-to place for all meats. They cut away the fat on roasts, steaks, etc., before they weigh them! Who does that? This is a no-frills operation, but then again, who needs Muzak and fancy parsley bordering day-old meat in semi-cold cases? Do bring cash or check only . . . don't hesitate [this place is] worth a trip to the North End."

ZUPPA DI PESCE

This is basically a fish stew, although sometimes it becomes a soup with a lighter broth. Any variety of fish and shellfish may be used. In each region of Italy fish stew takes a different name. In Tuscany it is called *cacciucco*; along the Adriatic coast it is *brodetto*. No matter what the name, it is a fish dish for any occasion. Most of the time it is served with a piece of crusty grilled bread and a bottle of red wine. It could also be served over *polenta*.

SERVES 4-6

3 tablespoons olive oil, plus extra for sautéing

1 tablespoon butter, plus extra for sautéing

1 medium onion, minced

2-3 cloves garlic, minced

Red pepper flakes to taste

1 cup dry white wine

1 (28-ounce) can diced tomatoes

1 tablespoon tomato paste

2 tablespoons fresh chopped basil

2 tablespoons fresh chopped thyme

2 tablespoons fresh chopped oregano

1-2 bay leaves

2 cups fish stock, or lobster stock if available

1 pound firm fish fillet (haddock, cod, or halibut), cut into large chunks, dusted with flour

½ pound mussels, scrubbed and debearded

12-14 clams

½ pound medium-size shrimp, peeled and deveined

Salt and pepper, to taste

Heat olive oil and butter in a large skillet over medium heat. Add onions and sauté until translucent.

Add garlic and pepper flakes, and cook for 2 minutes.

Add ¼ cup of the wine, and cook until wine evaporates.

Stir in the tomatoes, paste, herbs, remaining wine, and fish or lobster stock. Cover and simmer medium low heat for 20 to 30 minutes allowing flavors to blend.

Meanwhile in a skillet heat a small amount of oil and butter and briefly sauté the fish just enough to give it color. Set aside. It will add more flavors to the dish.

Recipe continues on page 158

When sauce is ready, add the mussels and clams, cover, and cook until they open. Discard any that do not.

Add the shrimp and fish. Simmer gently until shrimp and fish are just cooked through. Gently stir and cook for about 5 minutes longer.

Season with salt and pepper to taste. Ladle into warm bowls over a crusty piece of grilled bread.

COOK'S TIP: You may also steam the clams and mussels and use this as the stock in the recipe instead of fish or lobster stock. Discard shellfish that do not open. The shellfish should be added last to the recipe so they are not overcooked and just heated through.

DOLCE

Sweets

BISCOTTI OR "CANTUCCI"

Cantucci, or *biscotti,* are a type of cookie. A versatile traditional Italian holiday cookie, *cantucci* can be used as a garnish for most desserts.

MAKES ABOUT 20 BISCOTTI

2 cups all-purpose flour

1 cup sugar

1 teaspoon baking powder

⅛ teaspoon salt

3 large eggs

1 teaspoon almond extract

1 teaspoon vanilla

1 teaspoon anise extract

1 cup whole almonds, toasted and chopped a few times, not too fine

Preheat oven to 300°F.

Line 2 baking sheets with parchment paper

Combine dry ingredients and set aside.

Whisk the eggs, the almond, vanilla, and anise extracts using a mixer until well blended.

Add the dry ingredients, including the chopped almonds, and mix until combined. Dough should be thick and sticky at this point—DO NOT add more flour!

Scrape the dough onto a parchment-lined baking sheet. Flour your hands and shape dough into a long, flat loaf about 10 inches long and 5 inches wide. This will be kind of messy, so don't worry about how neat it is. Just try to form it into that general shape.

Bake until firm and dry, about 50 minutes.

Remove from the oven and allow to cool for 10 minutes. Then, using a long, serrated knife, slice loaf into ½-inch-wide slices. Lay the slices cut side down on the baking sheet and bake another 20 minutes. Turn slices over and bake 20 minutes more, or until the cookies are a light golden brown.

Cool the biscotti on a rack completely before storing in an airtight container until ready to serve.

BRAZADELLA (CIMBELLA)

I once learned to make this bread from my dear friend Mufalda (Muffie) Maioline. The way she cooked was typical of the way the Italian women in the village of Sagamore cooked. Muffie could not tell me the amounts of the ingredients she was using so to record the recipe, I had to measure everything. In her mind, there was no question as to the amounts she was using. She created the bread through instinct and intuition. Muffy passed away at age ninety-eight.

MAKES ONE BREAD AND SERVES 8

4 cups all-purpose flour

2 tablespoons baking powder

1 cup sugar

⅛ teaspoon salt

¼ pound (1 stick) butter, cut in small pieces

4 eggs, slightly beaten

1 cup raisins, soaked in warm water or whisky for 15 minutes

1½ ounces whiskey

1 teaspoon lemon extract

1 tablespoon vanilla

¼ cup milk

½ cup dense jam or mincemeat

1 egg

2 tablespoons milk

2 teaspoons sugar

Preheat oven to 350°F.

Butter and flour a 15-inch pizza pan or flat pan with sides.

In a large bowl, combine the flour, baking powder, sugar, and salt. With your fingers, work the pieces of butter into the flour mixture until granular in texture.

Turn the mixture onto a work surface and make a large well in the center. Put the eggs, raisins, whiskey, lemon extract, vanilla, and milk in the center. With a fork or with your fingertips, combine the liquid mixture with the flour until the ingredients are well incorporated and you can form a ball. Do not knead.

Cut the dough in half. With your hands roll it into two 2-foot-long rolls about 2½ inches in diameter. Take one roll, place it on the pan making a large ring, and seal ends together. With your fingers, make small indentations in the dough and fill each with jam or mincemeat. Place the second ring on top of the first.

Beat the egg with the milk and brush the rings with the mixture. Sprinkle with sugar and bake in a 350°F oven for 35 to 40 minutes. Test if it's cooked through with a cake tester.

BUDINO (CRÈME CARAMEL)

SERVES 6-8

½ cup sugar for caramel

2 teaspoons water

6 eggs

¼ cup sugar

2½ cups heavy cream

1 teaspoon vanilla extract

¼ cup whiskey

Put the sugar and water into a small, heavy saucepan and place it over medium-to-high heat and bring to a boil. Stir with a metal spoon until the sugar is a deep amber color and has caramelized. Then pour the mixture immediately into a soufflé dish, rolling the dish to coat both sides and bottom. Set aside.

In a bowl, combine the eggs with the sugar mixing until thick and lemon-colored. Gradually add the cream and vanilla; beat until blended. Pour egg mixture into soufflé dish and place it, covered, into a saucepan of boiling water for 30 to 35 minutes or until the tip of a knife inserted in center of custard comes out clean. Remove from the pan, pour whisky over the hot custard, and place on a rack to cool. Serve at room temperature or chill until ready to serve.

GOLDEN CANNOLI SHELLS COMPANY, INC.

99 Crescent Ave.
Chelsea, MA 02150
(617) 868-2826
goldencannoli.com

Since the second generation has taken over running the Golden Cannoli Shells Company, business has increased five-fold, and the company now turns out almost a quarter of a million hand-rolled cannoli shells every day.

Valerie Ann Bono is the company's vice president of sales and marketing. Her father, Francesco Bono, and his partner, Angelo Bresciani founded the company. Both men came to Massachusetts from Northern Italy, after a stopover of about a decade in Argentina. In the early 1970s the pair ran two Italian bakeries and, while they were renowned for their pastries, breads, coffees, and pizzas, they fried the popular cannoli shells in the back room of one of the bakeries. They began supplying not only their two bakeries, but other bakeries, with the cannoli. In 1978 they started Golden Cannoli Shells Company to keep up with the vast demand for the shells, which they now sell wholesale to an international market. In the early 1980s they sold the bakeries and their wholesale bread company, and focused exclusively on cannoli.

"Now we have the legacy of being a second-generation family business, which doesn't happen often," Valerie said. "And if it does, it's not very successful."

Valerie owns the company with her older sister, Marie Malloy, and Angelo's two sons, Eric and Ed Bresciani. A former Olympic-level hockey player at Providence College, Valerie joined the business in 2001 after deciding she didn't want to try to make a career of coaching girls in ice hockey.

"If you talk about being in love with your job and what you do, it's an understatement. I'm addicted to growing our family business," she said. "Our employees have been with us for twenty to thirty years. Some of them are still with us from when my father started the company."

In an industry that has been moving toward automation, Golden Cannoli has done the opposite and increased the number of employees. "We don't want to get rid of the human nature, the passion for the product," Valerie explained.

The company maintains a great tradition both in its products and in its customers. "The majority of our business is family business to family business," Valerie said. "It's kind of cool to see the generations that did business with my father are now doing business with me."

While Golden Cannoli produces the quick-fried shells, bakeries create their own fillings. The classic filling is made from ricotta cheese, confectioners' sugar, and vanilla extract. Variations on this include chocolate or caramel flavorings, but there are endless ideas for other types of fillings.

"A cannoli is definitely a treat that's far, far beyond the actual item," Valerie said. "It brings people together in ways that you can't imagine."

CANNOLI

MAKES ENOUGH FILLING FOR 12–14

1 cup whole milk ricotta, drained and squeezed dry

1 cup mascarpone cheese

½ cup confectioners' sugar

1 teaspoon pure vanilla extract

½ teaspoon cinnamon

Pinch of salt

¾ cup mini-chocolate chips, plus more for decoration (optional)

12 to 14 cannoli shells

Beat ricotta, mascarpone, confectioners' sugar, vanilla, cinnamon, and salt together until smooth. Fold in mini-chocolate chips. Cover and refrigerate for at least 1 hour.

Using a piping bag with an opening cut about the same diameter as the cannoli shells, fill each cannoli. Roll ends of each filled cannoli into the remaining mini-chocolate chips.

COOK'S TIP: Do not fill the cannoli shells ahead of time. The shells will get soft and chewy. You can make the shells and the cream ahead of time, but fill them shortly before serving.

TIRAMISU FOR DIPPING

This is a perfect holiday desert. Serve in small, fancy, glasses with *biscotti*. It will add to any festive event.

1 (8-ounce) container mascarpone cheese, softened

2 tablespoons confectioners' sugar

2 tablespoons instant espresso powder

1 (8-ounce) container whipping cream

1 tablespoon cocoa powder

Chocolate shavings for garnish

Biscotti for serving

In a medium-size bowl, beat the mascarpone, sugar, and espresso powder until smooth.

Whip the cream and fold most of it into the cheese mixture, reserving some for topping.

Divide the mixture and spoon into 6 small glasses and top each with a small dollop of remaining cream. Sprinkle with cocoa powder and shaved chocolate and serve with *biscotti* for dipping.

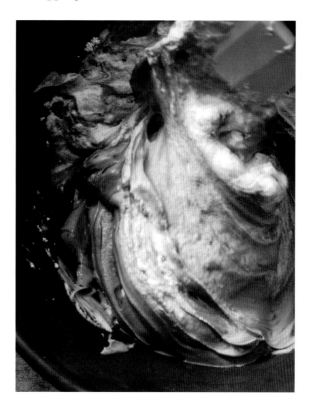

CITRUS OLIVE OIL CAKE

I have made this cake several times. It is wonderful served by itself or with a dollop of whipped cream. It can also be served with almonds, or sweetened raspberries or strawberries on the side.

FOR THE CAKE:

2
cups all-purpose flour

1¾ cups sugar

1½ teaspoons kosher salt

½ teaspoon baking soda

1½
teaspoons baking powder

1 cup extra-virgin olive oil

1¼
cups whole milk

3 large eggs

1 tablespoon each grated lemon and lime zest

½ cup combined fresh lemon and lime juice

1 teaspoon lemon extract

FOR THE GLAZE:

1 cup confectioners' sugar

1–3 tablespoons lemon juice.

FOR THE CAKE

Preheat the oven to 350°F.

Butter the sides of a 9-inch round springform cake pan and line the bottom with buttered or oiled parchment paper.

In a bowl, whisk the flour, sugar, salt, baking soda, and baking powder.

In another bowl, whisk the olive oil, milk, eggs, lemon and lime zest, juice, and lemon extract.

Add in the dry ingredients, and whisk until just combined. Do not over beat.

Pour the batter into the prepared pan and bake for 1 hour, until the top is golden and a cake tester comes out clean. Let cool for 30 minutes.

Remove sides of pan and let cake cool for several hours before serving.

FOR THE GLAZE

Mix confectioners' sugar with lemon juice. Drizzle over top of cake.

FISICHELLI'S PASTRY SHOP, INC.

55 Union St.
Lawrence, MA 01841
(978) 682-7774
fisichellispastryshop.com

Like most Italian enclaves, the church was the center of the community in Lawrence, Massachusetts. Italian immigrants first celebrated Mass in the basement chapel of the largely Irish St. Laurence O'Toole Church, at the intersection of East Haverhill and Newbury Streets. When they collected sufficient funds in 1909, they built the Holy Rosary Church nearby at the intersection of Union and Essex Streets. Most immigrants who lived in Lawrence were from Catania, Sicily. Many of the Italians who lived in the Newbury Street area had immigrated from Trecastagni, Viagrande, Aci Reale, and Nicolosi. They maintained a particular devotion to three Catholic martyrs—Saint Alfio, Saint Filadelfo, and Saint Cirino—and in 1923 began celebrating the Feast of Three Saints with a procession on their feast day. Although most of the participants live in neighboring towns, the Saints festival continues in Lawrence today.

My first stop in my research of this old mill town was the historical society. There I met a crew of friendly, helpful individuals with a lot of information about the town and its people. After going through pictures and files and selecting a few vintage pictures for this book, I ventured out into the streets to get a feel for the city. I was told about a popular nearby Italian pastry shop.

As I walked down Union Street, passing some of the older buildings that were once mills, I knew I had arrived at a special place when I saw a red-and-white-striped awning. When I opened the door I was greeted with the familiar smells of freshly baked Italian desserts. The cases were filled to the brim with cookies, pies, and pastries.

I had the opportunity to talk to the current owner, Nina Fisichelli (pronounced Fiz-a-kelly), about her personal history with Fisichelli's Pastry Shop. I learned that her grandfather, Orazio Fisichelli, came to Lawrence from Sicily and started the bakery in 1915. Nina explained how her grandfather baked bread and delivered it around the neighborhood with his horse and buggy. The horses were kept in a small stable a few blocks from the bakery. The original structure is still there but it is now an automotive shop

"I say to myself, that was once my grandfather's horse stables and I have fond memories when I pass it," she said.

In 1922 Orazio met Lena Gallo and they married. They both worked in the bakery in the 1920s and early 1930s during the Great Depression. They had two sons, Frank and Edward.

"When my father Frank was 12, he would help deliver the freshly baked bread throughout the City of Lawrence during the night," Nina said.

The bakery was taken over by her father around 1952, and he expanded the business by making pies, cream pastries, cakes, and his signature wedding cakes. In 1965 Frank and Muriel had their only child, Nina.

"I was always with my mother, at home and in the bakery. Everywhere she went, I went. We had quality time together."

At the age of 9, Nina lost her mother, and from then on spent most of her time in the bakery with her father, watching him make wedding cakes, pies and cookies.

"I used to take naps in one of the big breadbaskets."

Fisichelli's is well known for its 30 varieties of handmade Italian cookies, *biscotti*, and cakes, especially wedding cakes.

In 1991, Nina told me, her father wanted to retire. She was teaching grade school and studying for her master's degree in speech. Her father did not want her to take over the business because he knew how much work was involved.

"I guess it was my Italian guilt that kicked in. I was the only child and decided to take over the tradition or it all would be lost. At the time, I knew nothing about running the business except what I remembered seeing my father do," she recalled. "I have my own flare, different from his. My father was a real artist when it came to making those wedding cakes and handmade pastries."

Nina is now a third-generation Fisichelli, carrying on the family tradition as owner/operator of the 100-year-old business. She ships her cookies all over the United States, something her father resisted because, as she said, "He was Old World."

FISICHELLI'S ITALIAN ALMOND MACAROONS

3 egg whites

1 cup sugar

1 pound almond paste (about 1½ cups)

1½ cups sliced almonds

In the bowl of a large mixer, beat the egg whites until stiff peaks form. Gradually add the sugar, and beat until well combined and the peaks are glossy.

Break up the almond paste and add to the egg whites. Beat until well combined.

Roll the mixture into a large ball and chill for several hours or overnight.

Take a tablespoon of dough and roll it into an oblong shape.

Pour the almonds onto a small plate, then roll and press the almonds into the cookie dough, covering all sides.

Place on a cookie sheet lined with parchment paper and bake for 30 to 35 minutes until the almonds are slightly toasted, being careful not to burn them. The cookies should be cooked long enough to have a crunch.

COOK'S TIP: This recipe can easily be doubled.

BREAD AND ROSES

The Lawrence Textile strike on January 1, 1912, was known as the "Bread and Roses" strike. It was taken from the American poet, novelist, and editor, James Oppenheim's poem by the same title. The workers in Lawrence from many ethnic backgrounds lived in crowded and unsafe apartment buildings, often with many families sharing the same apartment. In the mills and factories men, women, and children worked long hours in unsafe conditions and were underpaid. Joseph Ettor of Industrial Workers of the World (IWW) had been organizing in Lawrence for some time before the strike. He and Arturo Giovannitti, a poet and union leader, assumed leadership of this famous strike.

When the strike started, the children of the laborers were shipped off to New York City. This followed the Italian custom—when there were lean times and strikes, children were sent off to family members and returned when things were quiet again. This reduced expenses for the strikers and it also generated public sympathy and financial support.

During the uprising, a women striker, Anna LoPisso, was shot and killed, possibly by police. Ettor and Giovannitti were charged with the murder even though they were 3 miles away at the time, speaking to another group of workers.

Jonas Stundzia, one of the founders of the Historical Center in Lawrence and chairman of the Lawrence Historical Commission, has been researching the Lawrence strike for more than 40 years.

"I was born in Lawrence and had the opportunity to interview elderly people who had a connection and history of the strike," he said. He explained that a third man, Giuseppe Caruso, was put in jail along with Etto and Giovannitti, but not much is known about him. Caruso was arrested in April and accused of the murder after it was made known that Ettor and Giovannitti had an alibi, Jonas said. Caruso was jailed with Ettor and Giovannitti who had been incarcerated since January. An activist known to the police, Caruso did not speak a word of English. During the trial, which took place in October, everyone realized he was used as the fall guy. During the trial Giovannitti gave such an eloquent and convincing speech of their innocence, the judge released all of them.

Other large strikes were taking place in the United States at that time. But, because the strike in Lawrence was such a powerful, massive event, with 25,000 participating from many ethnic groups, it was a tremendous victory for the IWW. It is still talked about today on many levels. One interesting fact is the people behind the strike, the organizers, were all Italian.

According to Sara, Arturo Giovannitti's daughter-in-law, "Arturo was extremely charismatic. The combination of his stage presence, enthusiasm, and passionate way of expressing himself made him a perfect candidate as a leader. He was also quite handsome. Later, his appearance became more theatrical. His style branded him; he wore a handmade Borsalino hat, dressed all in black with a flowing cape, a soft silk cravat tied around his neck. He used an elegant walking stick and was always seen with a large black dog trailing behind him. He was an artistic, aristocratic gentleman who fought for the working class.

In A Prison Cell Because
They Are Loyal To Their Class

TWO NOBLE FIGHTERS IN THE STRUGGLE OF TWENTY FIVE
THOUSAND STRIKING TEXTILE WORKERS WHOSE WAGES
AVERAGED LESS THAN SIX DOLLARS PER WEEK.

Our Fellow Workers
Arturo Giovannitti & Joseph J. Ettor

INTERNATIONAL PRINTING CO.

SAVOR, A VILLAGE TRADITION

Savor (pronounced sa-VOR) is a dense fruit condiment, much like apple butter, that works with sweet and savory dishes. It also embodies the taste and history of a fading Italian culinary scene on Cape Cod.

In 2003 I was traveling in Emilia-Romagna when I was in a home where a woman had a pot of savor on the stove. She called it marmelade, but I knew it as the savor of my childhood on the Cape.

Not many of us still remember the Little Italy of Sagamore Village, located across the canal where the mainland becomes Upper Cape Cod. One could hear many regional dialects in this area, but Sagamore's Little Italy mostly consisted of Northern Italian immigrants. Men like my grandfather made their own wine and women made sweet ravioli for the holidays.

Each fall, a handful of us Italian Americans on the Cape still make savor, not only as a tie to history but also as a dish that more than holds it own today. It can be used as a filling for fried ravioli, crostatas, and tarts. It can also be a condiment for meat. I like to spread it on slices of toasted Italian bread for breakfast.

In Italy, cooks use apples, pears, and quinces in their savor. On Cape Cod, my neighbors made savor by cooking down late-season fruits, including adding local cranberries, in homemade red wine. It's a process that takes time and patience. You need to select the ripest fruit for the most intense sweetness and flavor. The savor then needs to be cooked in six- to eight-hour spans, with overnight rests. Like other dishes that require long cooking, be aware that the danger of scorching increases with every hour of cooking. The old cooks used very low heat and watched it intently when it reached the last stages.

I don't use homemade wine. After reading Ilaria Gozzini Giacosa's introduction to classical Roman cuisine, A Taste of Ancient Rome,' I started using saba, unfermented boiled-down grape must, because it produces a more complex richness.

TIME: 12 HOURS OVER 2 DAYS
YIELDS 11 PINTS

6 large ripe pears, peeled and cored

6 large crisp apples, peeled and cored

6 large ripe peaches, peeled and pitted

1 pound Italian prune-plums or other plums, peeled and pitted

1 pound seedless red grapes

12 ounces fresh cranberries

12 pitted prunes

12 ounces pitted dried apricots

12 ounces dark raisins

Zest of 2 oranges, removed in strips and minced

1 bottle red wine or saba

1 quart red grape juice

1 quart cranberry juice

1 cup cooked peeled chestnuts

Cut pears, apples, peaches, and plums into coarse, 1-inch cubes. Combine in a nonreactive (like stainless steel), heavy-bottomed, 8-quart pot. Add all remaining ingredients except for the chestnuts, and mix well.

Place pot over high heat and bring to a boil. Immediately reduce heat to its lowest possible setting, and simmer, uncovered, for 6 hours. Remove from heat and allow to sit, loosely covered, at room temperature overnight. (Sugar and acid in mixture will keep it from spoiling.) The next day, uncover pot and again bring to a boil. Reduce heat to lowest possible setting, and simmer for 6 more hours. Toward the end of the cooking, stir frequently to prevent scorching.

Remove pot from heat; mixture will be very dark and thick. Place chestnuts in a food processor and process to a mealy puree. Stir into cooked mixture. While mixture is still hot, pour into sterile pint jars and seal according to manufacturer's directions. Savor may also be covered and refrigerated for up to 4 months, or frozen in tightly sealed containers, for up to 6 months.

SAVORING RHODE ISLAND

Johnston, RI 02919
(401) 934-2149
savoringrhodeisland.com

Born in Watertown, Massachusetts, into an Italian family of six children, Cindy Salvato is no stranger to food; it was a major ingredient in her upbringing. As a child, one of Cindy's jobs was to make her father's lunch to take to work. Later Cindy left college to pursue her career in the food world.

"I studied at the former International Pastry Arts Center in New York City," Cindy explains. "Later I came back to the Boston area and worked as a pastry chef in several good restaurants."

Cindy's career blossomed. For over 13 years, she taught at the International Baking and Pastry Institute at the College of Culinary Arts at Johnson & Wales University. In 2003 she was a finalist for the Award of Excellence as Teacher of the Year at the International Association of Culinary Professionals (IACP). During this time she was certified as an executive pastry chef with the American Culinary Federation. She also worked as a food stylist and senior culinary advisor for Mary Ann Esposito's PBS show *Ciao Italia*.

As a teacher, she had a creative way of inspiring her students—with food.

"Most of my students were 'party people.' Sometimes it was hard for them to attend an early morning class and make chocolate mousse," she recalled. "I used to use a tour to Federal Hill as incentive for them to come to class. I would say, 'Okay, if we have perfect attendance for one week, I will take you to Federal Hill to meet my friends and eat good food.'"

It worked. "On one of the excursions, I took them to Michele Torpor's Boston Food Tours. It was Michele who encouraged me to come up with a name and give tours of Federal Hill. Savoring Rhode Island was born. I have been doing this for the last 14 years."

Cindy's tours include the history of Federal Hill. She leads her groups into some of the oldest established shops and specialty food markets, where they sample a variety of Italian meats and imported cheeses, olive oil, and wine. Cindy explains that the most interesting part of Savoring Rhode Island has been "watching some of the oldest, most established shops and purveyors in Providence change."

GREAT ITALIAN AMERICAN FOOD IN NEW ENGLAND

ITALIAN PLUM CAKE

When the Italian prune plums arrive, Cindy Salvato says she runs down to the market to stock up. "My mouth starts to water as I envision this cake hot from the oven," she says.

SERVES 6-8

FOR THE DOUGH

¼ cup lukewarm water

2½ teaspoons dry active yeast

1 tablespoon sugar

2 cups all-purpose flour

1¼ teaspoons salt

1 large egg

1 stick (4 ounces) unsalted butter, softened

TO FINISH THE CAKE

12–14 Italian prune plums

⅓ cup all-purpose flour

½ cup light brown sugar

1 teaspoon salt

2 tablespoons butter, slightly softened

¼ cup blanched almond slices, lightly crushed

TO MAKE THE DOUGH

In a small bowl whisk together the warm water and the yeast and set aside.

Put the remaining ingredients in the bowl of a food processor fitted with the dough blade. Add the yeast mixture and pulse until a ball is formed; it will be sticky, but don't add any extra flour. Remove the dough from the processor, transfer into a lightly oiled bowl, cover the bowl with plastic wrap, and refrigerate overnight; it will rise only slightly.

TO FINISH THE CAKE

Adjust the baking shelf in the oven to the center and preheat to 400°F.

Remove dough from the refrigerator and set aside. Halve the plums, remove the stones, and set aside.

Prepare the crumb topping by blending together the flour, sugar, salt, and butter. Rub the mixture with your fingers until crumbly. Stir in the almonds and set aside.

Grease a 9-inch springform pan. Remove the dough from the bowl and on a lightly floured work surface, press the dough with your fingers into a 9-inch circle. Place the dough in the pan and, leaving a half inch border at the edge of the dough, arrange the plums snuggly, like fallen dominos, with the cut side up, in circles, over the surface of the dough.

Sprinkle on the crumb topping and bake for 40 to 45 minutes. The topping and crust should be a light brown and the juices of the plums should be running.

GELATO FIASCO

74 Main St., Brunswick, ME, (207) 607-4262
gelatofiasco.com

Gelato Fiasco was born when two savvy young business school graduates wanted to get out of the house construction business and into something new. During a brainstorming session, Bruno Tropeano, Jr., and Joshua Davis decided to explore developing a gelato business. Because his father immigrated from southern Italy in 1969, Bruno made many trips to Italy, where he sampled many authentic Italian gelatos.

They began their new venture by enrolling in a four-day gelato-making course in Long Island, New York. The course was sponsored by an Italian gelato ingredient company. They needed financing for their idea. After approaching several banks, one finally gave them a loan and they bought a hot process machine and ingredients, and began creating their own recipes.

When it came to naming the business, they discovered that the name "Bruno's" was already taken by a Maine restaurant, so that was out. Gelato Fiasco just seemed to have a ring to it, an Italian ring, in fact. And even though fiasco is "a comedy of error," Bruno said, "we liked the way it flowed." Bruno and Josh call themselves *gelatieri*—gelato makers.

Gelato Fiasco differs from other gelato makers in that 90 to 95 percent of gelato makers—both here and in Italy—begin with a premixed or powder base to which they add the dairy ingredients. Bruno and Joshua start with natural ingredients, such as wild Maine blueberries and Sicilian pistachios, and quality ingredients, such as Ghirardelli chocolate chips and homemade marshmallows. They buy their milk and cream from Maine dairy farms. Their goal has been to rediscover the techniques of the Old World Italian "masters of gelato" while inventing innovative new flavors such as Caramel Sea Salt Gelato and A Bee's Aphrodisiac Gelato (flavored with honey and lavender).

"We picked the super-rare awesome way that nobody does anymore," Bruno explained. "If you're not going to be the best at something, why would you do it?"

In 2007 the pair opened their Brunswick, Maine, flagship store. In 2009 they began selling their gelato through grocery stores. They are now in more than 3,000 stores nationwide and will also ship anywhere in the United States. In 2012 they opened a second store in Portland, Maine.

"Even from the beginning people would be like, 'Wow, I haven't had gelato this good since I was in Italy.' That was kind of nice," Bruno said. "Now a lot of the time, people are like, 'Wow, this is better than the gelato I had in Italy.' I'm like, 'Thank you.'"

TOMIE DEPAOLA

After an arduous six-week journey by ship from Italy in 1907, the first thing Tomie dePaola's grandmother did when she joined her husband in Fall River was enter her new kitchen and begin cooking for her husband, his cousins, and their children. "'I was so happy, I came to a nice house and cooked a big meal,'" Tomie remembers his grandmother Nona saying.

Tomie is an award-winning illustrator and author of nearly 250 children's books. His most famous book is *Strega Nona*, which means "Grandma Witch." Published in 1975, the book was a runner-up for a prestigious Caldecott Medal. Set in Calabria, the book tells the story of a magic pot of pasta that overflows, nearly flooding and destroying a town. The beloved character of Strega Nona appears in over ten of Tomie's books.

Tomie's grandfather, a cobbler and shoemaker, traveled to America from the village of dePaola in Calabria with his cousins. He was, for many years, a "bird of passage," returning to his wife in Italy with the money he earned in America. Eventually he saved enough money to purchase tickets for his wife and children to join him in Fall River.

"And she came over with, let me see, there were three boys and one girl, four children, and she was pregnant with my father," Tomie told me.

Nona was illiterate—she could not read or write Italian and knew no English. She and her children wore nametags on the trip to Boston, and finally ended up in the Fall River trolley station, where Tomie's grandfather collected them after he finished his day's work.

The family eventually moved to Meriden, Connecticut. This is where Tomie's father Joseph met his mother, Florence. Growing up, Tomie sat in his grandmother's kitchen—the largest room in the house—and observed her as she cooked. Like many great cooks, Nona never measured anything.

"She used the *quanta basta* method of cooking—just enough. I never saw her use a spoon, but she used her fingers, her hands, a cup or palmful of water. It was just amazing," Tomie said. " I loved it. But she would never give us a recipe. You just had

to watch it and quickly write things down. The food was very simple, but it was very plentiful."

Another interesting aspect of Nona's cooking was her use of olive oil. Instead of extra-virgin oil, she bought a mixture of olive and corn oil in large cans. She reserved the good olive oil to add, a few drops at a time, to the salad. She would also apply a little olive oil to her shoulders if she got a sunburn.

At Easter, Nona baked a wonderful Easter bread, which Mary Ann Esposito featured in one of her cookbooks. In 1994 Tomie appeared on Mary Ann's *Ciao Italia* television show and together they baked a dove-shaped bread known as *Columba di Pasqua*. Tomie now often shares his Southern Italian recipes on *Ciao Italia* and he is a co-author with Mary Ann and Bill Truslow, of the cookbook *Celebrations Italian Style: Recipes and Menus for Special Occasions and Seasons of the Year*.

Tomie studied illustration at the Pratt Institute of Art in Brooklyn, graduating in 1956. During his long career he has cast a fond look back at his large Italian family in many of his books, including *26 Fairmount Avenue*, a tale set during the hurricane of 1938, which was the 2000 Newbery Medal Honor Book. In his 1973 *Nana Upstairs & Nana Downstairs*, a memoir of his grandmother and great-grandmother, he introduces young children to the concept of death. And of course, from Strega Nona's pasta pot to treats for the holidays, the food Tomie remembers as a child features deliciously in the books.

Tomie had an adventuresome palate even as a child—he ate baked mussels and raw clams when he was five and six years old. Today, Tomie is a very distinguished-looking, merry gentleman, with a white beard and round glasses riding around in a convertible with his dogs.

WANDE

Guanti, pronounced wanti, is the Italian word for glove and *wande* is the name Tomie's grandmother gave to these well- known Italian Carnival pastries. The name of these light glove-finger or angel-wing shaped delicacies changes in Italy depending on the region.

MAKES ABOUT 2 ½ DOZEN

1 ¾ cups all-purpose flour

1/8 teaspoon salt

½ teaspoon baking powder

½ cup sugar

2 eggs, slightly beaten

2 tablespoons almond extract

1 teaspoon vanilla extract

Oil for frying

More confectioners' sugar for dusting

Sift the flour, salt, baking powder, and sugar into a large bowl.

Make a well in the center of the dry ingredients. Add the eggs, almond and vanilla extracts.

Start mixing the ingredients with a fork, until well mixed. Use your hands until all the flour is combined with the liquid and forms a ball of dough.

Lightly flour a large work surface with flour. Knead the dough like you would pasta dough for 5 to 8 minutes until you have an elastic consistency.

Cover with a bowl and let the dough rest for 30 minutes.

Cut off small sections of the dough a little at a time, (NOTE you may also use a pasta machine to do this) and roll out into a long ⅛ inch thick strip. Us a knife of a pastry wheel, cut the dough into about 9-inch-long and ½-inch-wide strips. Tie them into a loose knot and set aside. Continue until all the dough is used.

Heat the oil to 375°F.

Place the knots into oil, a few at a time, turning once until slightly browned. Remove with a slotted spoon; on paper to drain.

When cool dust with sugar. Store in an airtight container until ready to serve.

PANFORTE DI SIENA

This unusual Italian treat dates back to the thirteenth century. It was a desert I had eaten but never made until Gillian Riley author of *The Oxford Companion to Italian Food,* mentioned it to me. I decided to develop this recipe around the ingredients in Gillian's book,

MAKES 16 SERVINGS

BREADCRUMB PAN LINING

1 tablespoon cake flour

1 tablespoon fine bread crumbs

2 tablespoons ground almonds

FOR THE CAKE

1 cup almonds or hazlenuts toasted and coarsely chopped

½ cup plus 1 tablespoon cake flour

1 teaspoon plus ½ teaspoon ground cinnamon for dusting

¼ teaspoon ground coriander

¼ teaspoon cardamom

¼ teaspoon ground nutmeg

¼ teaspoon ground clove

½ cup honey

2 tablespoons butter

½ cup granulated sugar

½ cup candied citron, cut into small pieces

½ cup candied orange peel, cut into small pieces

Confectioners' sugar for dusting

TO MAKE THE BREADCRUMB PAN LINING

Butter a 6-inch springform pan. Cut a piece of parchment or rice paper to fit pan bottom. (If using Asian-style rice paper, wet the paper to make it easier to cut, then trim it to the correct size with scissors.) Brush paper with butter and fit into pan bottom. In a small bowl, combine cake flour, bread-crumbs, and almonds. Evenly dust and shake this mixture over sides and bottom, removing any excess.

TO MAKE THE CAKE

Preheat oven to 350°F.

Place nuts in a single layer in an ungreased shallow pan or rimmed baking sheet. Bake 15 to 20 minutes, shaking the pan once or twice during toasting to aid in even browning. When nuts are golden brown, remove them from oven and let cool.

In a bowl, combine ½ cup cake flour, 1 teaspoon cinnamon, coriander, cardamom, nutmeg, and cloves; set aside.

In another small bowl, combine remaining tablespoon cake flour and ½ teaspoon cinnamon. Set it aside for the topping.

In a medium saucepan over low heat, combine honey, butter, and sugar. Cook, stirring occasionally to prevent scorching, until mixture comes to a full boil. Remove from heat and stir in candied fruit and toasted nuts.

Sift in flour mixture; stir until well blended.

Pour batter into prepared pan. Smooth the top slightly and sift the reserved cinnamon-flour mixture over the top.

Place cake in center of middle oven rack. Bake for 30 to 40 minutes or until *panforte* just starts to simmer around edge of pan. Remove from oven; cool completely on a wire rack.

Remove sides of springform pan. Use a knife to peel away parchment or rice paper. Invert *panforte* again and transfer onto a wire rack. Dust top with confectioners' sugar and serve at room temperature.

COOK'S TIP: If saving cake for future use, do not dust with the sugar. It can be wrapped in several layers of plastic wrap and a layer of aluminum foil and stored in an airtight container for several weeks, or be frozen for up to six months.

QUINCE POACHED IN VIN SANTO AND SPICES

Quince is one of the most underutilized fruits. Most people poke them with clove and place them in their dresser draws to scent their cloths, or use them in jams and jellies. They are delicious as a dessert. Try this spiced quince after a rich or heavy meal.

SERVES 6-8

4 ripe quinces

1 lemon

3 cups Vin Santo

1½ cups water

¼–½ cup sugar

3 cardamom pods

1 cinnamon stick, broken

4 cloves

3-4 whole allspice

5-6 black peppercorns

Peel, quarter, and core the quince, reserving peels and cores. Place quince in a bowl with the juice from the lemon. Toss with the juice to prevent browning.

In a large saucepan, combine wine, water, and spices and bring to a boil then simmer, stirring with a wooden spoon to dissolve the sugar.

Add the quince, the peels, and the core to the sugar syrup. Cover and simmer on low heat for 1½ to 2 hours until quince is tender. Remove from stove and allow to cool.

Once cool, put the quince in a bowl. Strain the remaining syrup and return to the saucepan and reduce it to a thick consistency. It will also thicken as it cools. Pour the sauce over the quince, and serve warm with vanilla ice cream.

SCIALO BROS. BAKERY

275 Atwells Ave.
Providence, RI 02903
(401) 421-0986
sicalobakery.com

It was a damp, rainy, winter day when I entered this warm, friendly bakery. The charming room was filled with the smells and sights of beautiful Old World baked goods. There were lovely handcrafted Italian cookies, some filled with fruit others topped with nuts; cakes, including a marzipan-covered Sicilian cassata; and freshly backed breads. I met Lois Scialo Ellis at the counter and, as she was showing me through the bakery, she told me the story of how she and her sister Carol Scialo Gaeta, two well-educated women with lives of their own, came to own and operate

the oldest family-run business on the hill.

"In the early 1900s the bakery was started by my father Luigi and his brother," Lois explained. "They did not get along and my uncle went back to Naples, Italy, where he was from. It was my father Luigi's bakery from then on."

Lois went on to tell me her family history, about her father's two marriages and how they lived above the bakery.

"It was the summer of the 1938 hurricane. My father went to work, leaving his wife Alele Cilento and infant daughter in their summer home in Warwick, Rhode Island. That day, a tidal wave came up Narraganset Bay. He lost his wife and child in the storm." Lois continued her story. "Then in 1940 he married my mother Aassunta and with that marriage he had three daughters. My father died at the age of 103 and left the bakery to the three daughters, Lois, Carol, and Susan. My sister Carol and I tried to sell the bakery and the sale fell through. Our children encouraged us to not sell and keep the business going. We bought out our sister Susan and the two of us formed a partnership. We now carry on our family tradition in the bakery."

RED WINE BISCUITS

This is one of Luigi Scialo's favorite recipes. His red wine biscuits were sold in the store for many years.

4 cups all-purpose flour

1 cup granulated sugar

1 tablespoon baking powder

1 teaspoon salt

1 tablespoon aniseed

1 cup red wine

1 cup oil (corn or olive)

1 large egg

¼ cup water

Preheat oven to 350°F.

Prepare two cookie sheets with pan spray, a silicone mat, or parchment paper.

In the bowl of an electric mixer, blend flour, sugar, baking powder, salt, and aniseed. Add the red wine and oil on low speed. Mix until the dough comes together. It's important to not over mix the dough; it should NOT be smooth.

Remove dough from mixer, and cut into 4 equal pieces. Working with one piece at a time, roll the dough into an even, 8-inch log. You will not need any extra flour for rolling. Cut the log into 8 even pieces and roll each piece into a 7-inch log. Make each log into a ring and pinch the ends together; transfer to a prepared baking sheet. Repeat this procedure for the remaining dough.

This is rustic dough so, don't panic if it starts to open or split as you are rolling. Simply pinch it back together.

Whisk together egg and water. Brush the egg mixture onto each cookie.

Bake for 30 to 40 minutes until cookies are firm, they should not spring back.

Cool completely and store in an airtight container.

SALAME DOLCE DI CIOCCOLATO

Traditionally, this recipe called for the use of raw eggs, but I successfully adapted it without the eggs.

SERVES ABOUT 10-12 SLICES

6 tablespoons (¾ stick) unsalted butter, cut into ½-inch pieces

1 (1-ounce) bag semi-sweetened chocolate chips

¼ cup brewed coffee

1 cup slivered almonds, toasted

1½ cups cookies, such as *biscotti* or butter cookies, crushed

2 teaspoons dark rum

½ cup confectioners' sugar

Put the butter and chocolate in the top of a double boiler. Place the pan over medium heat and simmering water. Stir until the chocolate has melted and the mixture is smooth. Mix in the coffee until smooth, add the almonds, cookies and the rum.

Put the mixture into a medium bowl, cover, and refrigerate until firm but moldable, about 1½ hours.

Place the mixture in the center of an 18-inch long piece of parchment paper. With a spatula, form the mixture into a loaf that is approximately 3 inches in diameter by 8 inches long. Wrap in parchment paper, twist the ends to seal, and refrigerate until firm, about 1 hour

Spread confectioners' sugar on a cookie sheet, remove the parchment paper then roll the log in the sugar until coated. Let the log rest at room temperature for 10 minutes before cutting, then, using a sharp serrated knife, cut the log into ½-inch-thick slices and serve.

ALBA ROSSI

Alba Benedini Rossi is "ninety-eight and three quarters years old," as she put it! Both her parents came from Carrara, Italy, in 1911. One of her father's brothers, already working in the granite sheds in Vermont, told her father there was a lot of work here. "It was my father who came first," Alba recalled. "My mother followed him later." Alba said it took 30 days to cross the Atlantic Ocean to reach Staten Island in New York. "They couldn't speak English. A tag was put on them and they were shipped off to Vermont," she said. Alba and her siblings—three boys and three girls—were born in Barre, Vermont.

"My mother always spoke Italian to us. Both parents didn't speak much English. I love the Italian language, but I don't speak it very much anymore because there's nobody around to talk to," she said. "It's bad to lose a beautiful language like that."

When asked what foods her mother prepared when she was growing up, Alba said, "Our food was simple. Mostly during the week we would have soups. One day it was chicken broth. We had our own chickens and gardens," she recalled. "Sometimes it would be beef, potatoes, and a salad. Other times it was bean soup, pasta fagioli, or *pastasciutta*" (pronounced: pastashutta). Alba explained that *pastasciutta* is pasta generally served with sauce and not broth.

Only on Sunday did Alba's mother make dessert and it was usually something like a *torta di riso*. She checked to make sure I knew what that was. I did.

As we continued our conversation, I asked Alba if she had any old pictures of her family she could share with me. She told me, "I am almost 99 years old and I am losing my eyesight, so it is very difficult for me to look up things now. I do use a magnifying machine, but my eyes get tired quite easily." I told her I understood. The sharpness and clarity with which she remembered things from her childhood amazed me. It will be one of the memories in writing this book I will cherish. Thank you, Alba Rossi.

TORTA DI RISO (RICE CAKE)

Alba Rossi's recipe, which has many variations, is a dense, rich rice cake best when served with a dollop of slightly sweetened whipped cream. Making this dessert the day before allows the flavors to marinate. It can be made either in two 7-inch springform pans that make smaller cakes, or one large pan that takes longer to bake, but results in a higher cake.

ONE CAKE SERVES 6-8.

3½ cups milk

1 cup imported Arborio rice

2 teaspoons butter

Bread crumbs for dusting pans

5 large eggs

1¼ cups sugar

1 teaspoon almond extract

1 teaspoon vanilla

1 tablespoon grated lemon zest

¾ cup candied citron, finely diced

½ cup almonds, toasted and coarsely chopped

Whiskey

In a heavy 3- to 4-quart saucepan with cover, combine milk and rice. Bring to a gentle boil over high heat. Turn heat to low, cover tightly, and cook about 20 minutes, stirring occasionally to check for sticking. The rice should be a little tender but still resistant to the bite. The mixture will also be a little soupy. Turn into a large bowl and allow to cool.

Butter two (7-inch) springform pans, dust with breadcrumbs and set aside.

Preheat oven to 350°F.

Beat eggs and sugar with an electric beater until well combined. Add the almond extract, vanilla, and lemon zest. Pour egg mixture into the cooled rice and fold in the citron and almonds.

Divide the mixture between the two prepared springform pans, and bake for 45 to 55 minutes, or until a knife inserted in the center comes out clean. Remove from oven and pour generous amounts of whisky over the cakes. Allow to cool on a rack, then unmold and serve at room temperature topped with a little whipped cream.

POLCARI'S COFFEE

105 Salem St.
Boston, MA 02113
(617) 227-0786
polcari'scoffee.com

When Polcari's Coffee opened in 1932 in Boston's North End, it "catered to poverty." Now owner Bobby Eustace says, "We weren't catering toward the rich and famous. We were trying to help the poverty in the area. It was all poverty."

This was the Great Depression, and there were many years of hardship still to go. Polcari's carried lentils, beans, raw coffee, and rice.

"We were selling basically *polenta*," Bobby said. "At the time we had ham hocks. We were doing dried sausages—anything cheap. As people came in here, they wanted stuffed peppers, so we carried them."

Anthony Polcari, who came from Italy at age 20, had a dream to own a coffee shop. He saved his money while working as a pocket-maker at a local tailor's shop. After he opened the shop, his wife Rose and their children Ralph, Anthony, and Marie all worked in the store. Ralph eventually took over. Ralph, who had no children, became a mentor to Bobby when Bobby went to work at the store full-time. When Ralph passed away, Bobby took over.

Coffee has, of course, always been a mainstay of the business. Today while Polcari's sells Blue Mountain and Hawaiian Kona coffees, Anthony Polcari's house blend (a mixture of dark and light roasts) and Italian roast (espresso) remain store favorites.

"We used to roast our coffee back in the day," Bobby said. In the 1940s or 1950s Polcari's stopped roasting its own coffee because larger companies could roast it for just about the same price.

"At the time we didn't care who did it, as long as it was done. Nowadays, we still have the same company we have been with since the 1960s, they still roast our coffee. They are always on point."

Today the store remains proud of its Old World flavor. It sells Italian hard candy, pasta, beans, nuts, coffee, and tea as well as their famous herb mixture for dipping bread.

"So basically, the store was once in poverty, and now we do have a $30 bottle of vinegar, but we might not sell it for a week," Bobby said. "Our average sale is about $6."

ESPRESSO GELATINA CAFFÈ (ESPRESSO COFFEE JELLY)

1 (¼-ounce) package unflavored gelatin

4 tablespoon sugar

3 tablespoons cold water

2 cups fresh brewed espresso coffee

In a small saucepan, combine gelatin, sugar, and cold water. Add 1 cup of the coffee and boil over high heat. Stir until the gelatin and sugar have dissolved. Pour the mixture into a small bowl with remaining coffee, cover with plastic wrap, and chill in the refrigerator until solidified about 6 hours.

INDEX

INDEX

ACKNOWLEDGMENTS

For most of my life I have been working on this project collecting recipes, photos and other relative material from the people in the village. A long time supporter with a wealth of information was Barbara Gill Archivists, Sandwich Library. Barbara has kept a file of periodicals and my history through the years. Also, Colleen Hayes and Lauren Robinson at the library's reference desk who filled my office with books and reference material for all requests. At The Bourne Historical Society, Gloria Dimock, Photo Archivisits, supplied me with several vintage photographs from the archives. As I ventured out to the towns and villages in the six New England states, the list grew. I want to thank the wonderful people; some became friends, who invited me into their homes, kitchens and stores for the personal interviews in this book. Thanks to the Lawrence Historical Society, where I met Jonas Stundzia who sheared a wealth of information on the 1912 Lawrence Textile strike. Then on to the Vermont Historical Society in Barre and with the guidance of Paul Carnahan, Librarian and Marjorie Strong, his assistant, I was able to go through old photos of the quarries, manuscripts and even menus from many of the functions from Old Italian clubs in that region. I also thank the Springfield Historical Society and Danbury Museum and Historical Society for suggesting books and essays on Italian history. I also would like to acknowledge Claudia Tassinari, Assessor to Culture and Tourism, Cento Italy for her friendship, connection and passion for helping keep the Italian spirit and tradition alive on both sides of the ocean.

Un grande gratitudine e ringraziare to my dear creative colleague and friend Francine Zaslow for the time we spent together "playing with food." And Deb Johnson, Francine's efficient studio producer for organizing files, retouching photos to make the images special.

And I give recognition to the watchful eye of Debra Lawless, checking and helping me meet my demanding deadlines.

This book would never have happened if it wasn't for my editor Amy Lyons who believed in my project. Again, like with *Cape Cod Chef's Table,* she let me fly and be creative.

PS: A special "note" to John Murelle who brings music to our table.

ADDITIONAL PHOTO CREDITS

ABOUT THE AUTHOR

John F. Carafoli is an international food stylist, consultant, and food writer. His books include the seminal *Food Photography and Styling, Cape Cod Chef's Table,* and two children's cookbooks: *Look Who's Cooking* and *The Cookie Cookbook.* He has been published in *Gastronomica*, the *Journal of Food and Culture*, the *New York Times*, the *Boston Globe,* and *Edible Cape Cod* where he won an EDDY for Best use of Recipes in a Feature. He has been profiled in the Italian publication of *ER* (Emilia Romagna). In addition to presenting papers at the Oxford Symposium on Food and Cookery in England, he has organized the biannual International Conference on Food Styling and Photography at Boston University. Carafoli was featured on the NPR and Food Network's Ultimate Kitchens. He also conducts culinary, music, and culture tours to Italy. Carafoli lives in West Barnstable, Massachusetts and can be found in the waters during the winter months gathering fresh oysters and clams. Visit him at www.carafoli.com.

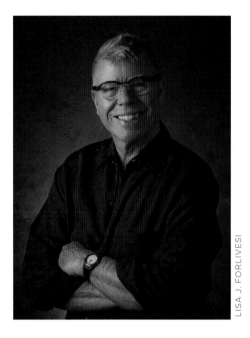

LISA J. FORLIVESI